MIDAS TOUCH

WHY SOME ENTREPRENEURS GET RICH– AND WHY MOST DON'T

DONALD J. TRUMP AND ROBERT T. KIYOSAKI

MIDAS TOUCH

WHY SOME ENTREPRENEURS GET RICH– AND WHY MOST DON'T

DONALD J. TRUMP AND ROBERT T. KIYOSAKI

PLATA
PUBLISHING

Photographs courtesy of Scott Duncan.
Published by Plata Publishing, LLC

Trump, Trump Organization and Trump University are trademarks of The Trump Organization. CASHFLOW, Rich Dad, Rich Dads Advisors, ESBI, B-I Triangle are registered trademarks of CASHFLOW Technologies, Inc.

Some of the company and product names mentioned in this book are the trademarks or registered trademarks of their respective companies. They were used for identification purposes only.

   are registered trademarks of
CASHFLOW Technologies, Inc.

Plata Publishing, LLC
4330 N. Civic Center Plaza, Suite 100
Scottsdale, AZ 85251
(480) 998-6971

Visit our websites: PlataPublishing.com, Trump.com, RichDad.com
Printed in the United States of America
First Edition: August 2011
ISBN: 978-1-61268-095-8

Dedication

---

*To the entrepreneurs of today who struggle, strive, and succeed
and to the entrepreneurs of tomorrow who will see opportunities
where others see only obstacles...*

*Visionaries all who act boldly and leave their unique imprint,
their Midas Touch,
on the economic landscape of our world.*

Also by
Donald J. Trump and Robert T. Kiyosaki

Why We Want You To Be Rich
Two Men • One Message

Authors' Notes
and Acknowledgments

We would like to thank all the people who contributed to our lifelong passion of entrepreneurial learning. Without them this book, which is based on our experiences, would not have been possible.

We'd also like to acknowledge our wins and our losses, our successes and our failures because, without life's balance of ups and downs and the personal and professional growth that comes with it, we would not be where we are today.

A special thank-you goes to Meredith McIver and Kathy Heasley who provided editorial assistance. Special thanks as well to Allen Weisselberg, Michael Cohen, Rhona Graff, Jonathan Gross, and Kacey Kennedy at The Trump Organization and Mike Sullivan, Marian Van Dyke, Anita Rodriguez, Michael Joe, Rhonda Hitchcock, and Mona Gambetta at The Rich Dad Company and Plata Publishing. Their collaborative efforts and entrepreneurial insights helped bring our vision of *Midas Touch* to life.

Finally, we'd like to thank all the entrepreneurs who are innovating, risking and overcoming every hurdle to better their lives, their families' lives and the lives of billions of people around the world.

There is nothing more noble than entrepreneurship, and we applaud you for your efforts, for your success and for your contributions to our world.

FOREWORD
by Mark Burnett

Entrepreneurs have a singular drive that gets them where they're going. It's a focus that is so intense that nothing can derail them or their plans.

Years ago, long before meeting Donald, I read his first book, *The Art of the Deal*. At the time, I was selling T-shirts on the beach in Los Angeles. In between customers, I was constantly reading *The Art of the Deal*. I especially appreciated that it was written for someone like me—someone who had never been to business school. I was in total awe of this real estate mogul, Donald Trump, and never believed I would set eyes on the man himself, let alone meet him. I certainly never imagined that I would be in business with him.

One of the most memorable stories I can remember from *The Art of the Deal* was the story about how Donald can spot "a loser." He explained that a loser is the person with a for-sale sign on a dirty car. While this seems obvious, it's amazing the number of people who do exactly this in various ways in various businesses.

Robert has sold well over 30 million books in countries all over the world. He obviously has a message that people want or need to hear. He sees himself primarily as a teacher, and I admit that I see Donald as a teacher as well. *The Apprentice* has an educational subtext that he taps into very well, and I think it's one reason the TV show has had the resonance and longevity that it has had. These two teachers, these two titans of business, have a message for all of us.

As *Midas Touch* points out, entrepreneurship is something that has become somewhat of a responsibility these days, or should be. That's why this book is timely. We need people who have the talent to create jobs. Those who have the skills or ability to be an entrepreneur need to develop these skills in order to contribute to our society. This book comes from two highly accomplished entrepreneurs with very different backgrounds who cover the bases from different perspectives.

Anyone wanting to enter the leagues of entrepreneurship should give this book a thorough read.

Entrepreneurs are characterized by singular focus and powerful drive. I saw that aspect of Donald a long time ago, and Robert has it as well. I can tell you that their drive is palpable. They don't stop, and the successes they have achieved are remarkable. I hope you will take the time to listen to what they have to say.

DREAMER... OR ENTREPRENEUR?

One entrepreneur, a mechanically minded man since childhood, saw his chance to change the world. He saw a way to better it for people everywhere. So he set out, not to build his fortune, but to build his dream of a new way of life for everyday people.

He struggled with the challenges of honing his idea, prototyping countless versions of his product—each one a slight improvement over the last—and building his company. But his greatest struggle was with people who couldn't see his vision, who couldn't expand their focus and see things as they could be, rather than as they were. The battles were many, but he kept going. He doubted himself, made plenty of sacrifices along the way and got sidetracked many times. He failed often and, because he always loved famous sayings, he called failure "the opportunity to begin again—more intelligently."

He wasn't a good student and learned very little in school, but he did love to take things apart to see how they worked. "Dismembering watches" was a favorite pastime. He had no advanced degree, but he did attend night school to hone his skills. His mind was brilliant, and eventually he became a much-loved teacher of his craft. He attracted students who, like him, were enthusiasts. In the late hours of the night, they would volunteer their time to work on projects and learn in the process. His ability to attract talent and work with others was enviable. In his business, he surrounded himself with people who knew what he did not.

He succeeded at raising money from investors who believed in his product. The problem was that they didn't always believe in his vision. He grew despondent because they only focused on money. At one point, he was fired from his own company, the company that bore his name. A lesser man would have called it quits and found a job.

Years earlier, he had given up a steady job with a prominent company. Entrepreneurship didn't pay very well so his family moved countless times into ever more modest surroundings. Ironically, while still working his day job, inspiration came from his iconic employer, a man he had idolized from childhood and had the honor to meet one day, just for a moment. In a few quick strokes, he sketched his innovation. The man before him pounded his fist on the table and said, "Young man, that's the thing. You have it. Keep at it."

"That bang on the table was worth worlds to me," the entrepreneur told his patient wife. "You won't be seeing much of me for the next year." In truth, success took more than a year. It took decades.

Answers rarely come through a eureka moment, and they didn't for Henry Ford. He observed the world around him and slowly arrived at his opportunity and his purpose. He demonstrated that an entrepreneur need not be the inventor of a new technology. His wild success came through something more valuable—a brand. Custom-made cars, the standard of the time, didn't align with Henry Ford's view of the world. He wanted to give *everyone* a luxury only the rich could then afford.

He wanted to change the world and believed the secret was an automobile with a gas combustion engine, assembled in a factory, where one car was the same as the next. His hero and famous employer, Thomas Edison, believed that too. That's why he pounded his fist on the table, reinvigorating Henry and prompting him to keep going through many years and many failures.

Henry dared to dream big. One Sunday he heard his minister preach, "Hitch your wagon to a star," and he told his sister, "That's what I'm going to do." That was in 1893. Ten years later, on July 23, 1903, Chicago dentist Dr. Ernst Pfenning bought Ford Motor Company's very first Model A.

Henry Ford had done it. No longer a dreamer, he was an entrepreneur.

CONTENTS

STRENGTH OF CHARACTER
TURNING BAD LUCK INTO GOOD LUCK

F.O.C.U.S.
FOLLOW ONE COURSE UNTIL SUCCESSFUL

BRAND
WHAT YOU STAND FOR

RELATIONSHIPS
YOU CAN'T DO A GOOD DEAL WITH BAD PARTNERS

LITTLE THINGS THAT COUNT
WHAT SUCCESSFUL ENTREPRENEURS DO THAT OTHERS DON'T

GUIDE TO DEVELOPING
YOUR MIDAS TOUCH
DONALD J. TRUMP & ROBERT T. KIYOSAKI

INTRODUCTION
Entrepreneurs are Different

This is a book about entrepreneurs, and what makes entrepreneurs different. This is a book for those people who are already entrepreneurs or for those who would like to be.

This is not a textbook written by college professors who teach entrepreneurship. It doesn't paint a rosy picture or provide a clinical, step-by-step path to success. Both are unrealistic, and this book is very realistic. That's because it's a book written by entrepreneurs who have won, failed, and battled back to win, again and again. And in it, we openly tell our stories.

The entrepreneur's ability to dream, win, lose, and win again and again is often called *entrepreneurial spirit*. It is what separates the entrepreneur from everyone else in business. It is also what separates those who want to be entrepreneurs from those who can be entrepreneurs.

This book has been in the works for nearly three years. We have continued our efforts on it because we both believe that only entrepreneurs create real jobs. And when the world experiences unprecedented levels of unemployment, jobs are what this world needs.

Chronic unemployment causes social unrest which can lead to revolution. The 2011 riots in the Middle East are cases in point. They are uprisings fueled by people who are willing, capable and eager to work, but who lack opportunity. They live in societies with chronically high unemployment. China shudders at the thought of their exports slowing and is horrified at the possibility of millions of unemployed workers. The U.S. government shares similar concerns and spends billions attempting to create jobs through government legislation and programs.

The problem is that no government, neither ours nor theirs, can create real jobs. Only entrepreneurs can do that. Only entrepreneurs can see the future and bring it to life—risking, losing, and winning—over and over. In the process, they create new industries and opportunities for people all over the world.

Another problem is that schools do not create entrepreneurs. Schools are designed to create employees. That is why people say, "Go to school to get a good job." Most students, even graduates of MBA programs, go on to become employees, not entrepreneurs. Millions of students leave school each year saddled with massive student-loan debt, unable to find jobs. Today, too many people, young and old, are looking for jobs, or are afraid of losing their jobs. We need more entrepreneurs who can create businesses and jobs.

Since the market crash that began in 2007, the biggest crash since the Great Depression, many have been waiting for the economy to come back. The economy will come back, but it will not be the same economy. The old economy of the Industrial Age is dying, and a new economy of the Information Age is emerging. The rules of this new economy, an international economy, will not be the same. And the old ideas from the Industrial Age—job security for life, pensions, benefits, and labor unions—will not be able to survive in our new Information Age.

Many of today's Fortune 500 businesses that were born in the Industrial Age will fade away. The Fortune 500 companies of tomorrow will emerge from this crisis, led by a new era of entrepreneurialism and a new class of entrepreneurs.

This book is written for these entrepreneurs and for the people who want to become these entrepreneurs. This book is not about business. It is about what it takes to become a successful entrepreneur.

As entrepreneurs, we share with you our thoughts and beliefs, our wins and our losses all accumulated over decades. You will learn what makes us succeed, when 9 out of 10 entrepreneurs fail. We will share how we managed to go beyond success and wealth, turning our businesses into international brands, a feat many entrepreneurs dream of, yet few achieve. More importantly, we share with you what keeps us going when others give up, and why we seek greater challenges. In this book, our second together, we share what gives us the Midas Touch, the ability to turn the things we touch into gold, and how you can have it too.

We've divided this book into five chapters, each one representing one of the five fingers of the Midas Touch hand. In each chapter, following our individual stories, we've included a "Distilling It Down" section that delivers an objective review of the key points. "Points to Remember | Things to Do" completes each chapter with action items you can apply to your own life.

The five fingers represent the five key factors every entrepreneur dreaming of success must master. These factors are not taught in school.

The Midas Touch hand is the ideal metaphor to represent the attributes critical to entrepreneurial success. Master every finger, and you'll discover the magic of why some entrepreneurs are wildly successful, and why most are not.

The thumb stands for strength of character. Without it, entrepreneurs cannot withstand the inevitable failures and disappointments that come with creating something out of nothing. Uncharted territory is full of dangers.

The index finger stands for focus. Entrepreneurs must have the proper focus to really succeed.

The middle finger, the longest finger, is all about the brand, which reflects what you stand for. Without a solid brand and a willingness to let the world know about it, you won't have the Midas Touch.

The ring finger is about relationships: how to find a good partner, be a good partner, and build different types of relationships to achieve success.

Finally, the little finger is about the little things. It's not about simply mastering the details. You will see that little things can become big things that can set you on a course of exponential success. You will learn how to find the little thing that can become a big thing for your customers and for your business.

Each of these factors is important on its own. Together, when all the awareness, skill, learning, and knowledge are in your hands, that's when the true Midas Touch power really shines. And our world could use some entrepreneurial shine. In fact, to solve the global problems of unemployment and the lack of job security and financial security, the world needs more entrepreneurs. We particularly need more wildly successful Midas Touch entrepreneurs.

Donald J. Trump   Robert T. Kiyosaki

CHAPTER ONE

THE THUMB
STRENGTH OF CHARACTER

"Life is like a grindstone. Whether it grinds you down or polishes you up depends on what you're made of."

– Anonymous

Turning Bad Luck into Good Luck
Robert Kiyosaki

In early 2000, I was in the Australian outback, far from civilization, on vacation with some friends, roughing it in one of the most beautiful parts of the world. It had taken me nearly a week to get to the remote campsite in Australia.

One evening, my satellite phone rang. It was my wife Kim, who was back home in Phoenix.

"Guess what?" she asked excitedly. "Oprah's producer called, and Oprah wants you on her program in Chicago."

"That's great," I replied. "But why me?"

"She wants to talk about your story and your book, *Rich Dad Poor Dad.*"

"That's good," I said. "Keep me posted."

"She wants you on her program in a few days."

"In a few days?" I moaned. "I just got here. Do you know how long it took me? Two days of flying and almost four days of driving. Can't we schedule it for a later date?"

"No. We've worked really hard to answer all their questions. The producer even called rich dad's son to verify that the story of your two dads was true. They're excited, and they want you now." Kim paused before continuing, "Don't pass this up. Just turn around. You'll have new tickets waiting for you at the Sydney airport."

Six days later, I arrived in Chicago.

Oprah's program was televised from her own studio, Harpo Productions. A lovely young assistant escorted me from the green room into the studio where Oprah's adoring fans were already seated.

The room was electric. Oprah's fans were anxiously awaiting her entrance. For a moment, I forgot why I was there. I forgot that I was about to be on television with the most powerful woman in show business. I knew her television viewership was estimated to be over 20 million people in the United States alone, with syndication in over 150 countries around the world.

Gazing around, I saw two chairs in the middle of the stage. I thought to myself, "I wonder who the second chair is for?" My heart froze as I realized... the second chair was for me!

The room suddenly erupted with applause as Oprah took the stage. She was much more impressive in real life. After she said a few words to the studio audience and her television viewers, the assistant gently took my elbow and said softly, "Let's go."

I took a breath and thought to myself, "It's too late to start practicing."

An hour later, the program was over. The crowd applauded, and Oprah said good-bye to the world. Once the television cameras were turned off, she turned to me, pointed, smiled, and said, "Rich dad, I just sold you a million copies of your book."

At that time, *Rich Dad Poor Dad* was self-published. This meant I did not have to share my profits with a publisher. Although I've never been good at math, I did understand money. After expenses, I made a profit of five dollars on every book. If Oprah's estimate was correct about selling a million copies of the book, simple math told me I just made $5 million in one hour, before taxes. It was a profitable day in many ways. I didn't know it at the time but, in one hour, I had gone from being an unknown to becoming world-famous. As you probably know, fame can be much more seductive than money.

The reason I self-published *Rich Dad Poor Dad* was because every publisher I sent it to turned it down. Most publishers were polite, but simply told me they had no interest in the book. Two sounded like my English teachers telling me I needed to learn how to write. One publisher said, "Your story is preposterous! No reader will ever believe it." And an editor who specializes in financial books rejected it, saying, "You don't know what you're talking about." He was referring to my lesson in *Rich Dad Poor Dad* where I stated, "Your house is not an asset." Of course, after the subprime crisis, millions of foreclosures, and all the homes that are worth less than their mortgages, I wonder if that editor would reconsider my message in *Rich Dad Poor Dad.*

Taking the rejection in stride, Kim and I self-published 1,000 copies of the book and quietly released it at my birthday party in April 1997.

From 1997 to 2000, *Rich Dad Poor Dad* grew by word of mouth. Friends would hand it to friends, and friends would give it to family members. The book slowly climbed its way to *The New York Times* bestseller list, the only self-published book on the list at the time. Oprah's producer called shortly after the book made *The New York Times* bestseller list. Ten years later, in 2010, I estimated that Oprah's push helped me sell over 22 million copies of *Rich Dad Poor Dad* in over 100 countries. The book has now been translated into more than 50 languages. That is the power of Oprah.

Immediately after the show aired, the press came to call. Most loved the simple story of my two dads. A few were skeptical, critical, or condemning.

Failure Leads to Success

Several TV hosts and magazine articles labeled me an "overnight success." Every time I heard or read those words, I chuckled. While it was true that I went from obscurity to world-famous in one hour,

I was hardly an overnight success. In 2000, I was 53 years old. For most of those 53 years, I was far from successful.

Thomas Edison, inventor of the light bulb and founder of General Electric, once said, "I haven't failed. I've found 10,000 ways that don't work."

Edison's quote summarizes why most people fail to become successful entrepreneurs. The quote also explains why most entrepreneurs fail to develop their Midas Touch. Simply put, most people fail to become successful because they fail to fail enough.

Relative to the Midas Touch, the thumb represents your emotional maturity and strength of character. Without the thumb, the other four fingers lack the stability to handle the daily challenges, the ups and downs, wins and losses, that all entrepreneurs face every day.

What Do You Lack?

Many people say that two things stop most new entrepreneurs:

1. The lack of capital
2. The lack of real-life business experience

From my own experience, I would add a third item:

3. The lack of emotional maturity and strength of character

Of these, I believe the third one, the lack of emotional maturity and strength of character, is the main reason why people fail as entrepreneurs.

The world is filled with smart, well-educated, talented people who fail to develop their God-given talents or gifts. How often does the student voted "Most Likely to Succeed" fail to succeed? Most of us know people whose lives are tales of woe, tragedy, or betrayal, who blame their failures on other people or on a bad start in life. We all know people who have great ideas about how to make millions of dollars, but are too lazy to get off the couch. We all know people who live in the future, and fail to take action today. There are millions of people who want to change the world, but cannot change the conditions of their own lives. And we all know people who lie, cheat, and steal, and yet lie again to themselves, believing they are people of integrity. Without the emotional maturity and strength of character represented by the thumb, most people are denied access to their Midas Touch.

If I Had Known Then What I Know Now...

When speaking to a group of "wanna-be" entrepreneurs, I often begin by saying, "If I had known how much I did not know, I might not have started." I also say, "If I had known how hard it was going to be, I might not have started." To give these budding entrepreneurs some "brightness of future" though, I usually add, "I'm glad I did not know, because if I did, I might not be successful today." I then begin to tell them about my failures, because failure was my path to success.

Don't Read Any Further

In the following pages, I will share a few real-life experiences about pain and failure. Why do I want to tell you about my pain and failure? The answer is simple. If my pain and failure discourage you from becoming an entrepreneur, then I have done you a big favor.

While almost everyone has the *ability* to become an entrepreneur, not everyone *needs* to become an entrepreneur. There are easier ways to live your life.

Life and success seem easy for some people, but I do not know any of these people. As my rich dad often said, "Success requires sacrifice." I have yet to meet a successful person who did not sacrifice tremendously for that success. For example, medical doctors pay a steep price in terms of time, money, energy, and relationships to become doctors. So do most high-performance athletes, movie stars, music idols, political leaders, and social leaders. Success in business is no different.

Sacrifice is the price a person pays for success. Unfortunately, most people are not willing to pay the price. It is easier to be average, comfortable, safe, secure, and live life just below success.

Stories of My Own Stupidity

Albert Einstein once said: "Only two things are infinite—the universe and human stupidity. And I'm not sure about the former."

I am living proof of Einstein's insight. My stupidity is infinite.

The following are examples of my stupidity when I started my first business called Rippers, a nylon-and-Velcro surfer-wallet business, which grew into a big business. To preface the story, I had started a number of smaller businesses before creating Rippers, but none had taken me to an international level as the nylon-wallet business did. The interesting thing is that I did not want to be in the nylon-wallet business. I fell into the business through my stupidity.

Story #1: A Fool and His Money

As most people know, the number-one skill of an entrepreneur is the ability to sell, because *sales equals income.* Since I did not know how to sell, I took my rich dad's advice and got a job working for the Xerox Corporation at the age of 26, not because I liked copiers, but because Xerox had a great sales-training program. Although I was not good in sales, I studied, practiced, took extra classes, and slowly but surely, after three years, was consistently one of the company's top sales agents and actually started making some money. From 1974 to 1976, I managed to save $27,000 (which back then was a lot of money) to start my first business.

There is a saying that goes: "A fool and his money are soon parted." Well, I was the fool, and my money was soon gone. This is how I parted with my money.

A friend called me to ask if I would invest in his company. He promised I would have the money back in a month plus 20% interest. My friend John had been a very successful entrepreneur (emphasis on the words "had been"). So I believed he was smart, successful, and would take care of my money for 30 days. Besides that, a 20% return on my money was tempting. So, I handed him the money, and he handed me back a promissory note.

A month later, I called John to collect my $27,000 plus $5,400 in interest. As you may have already guessed, he did not have the money. He blamed his CFO, Stanley, a CPA by training, for the mix-up.

"I told Stan to buy more product so we could ship it to our retailers," said John, "but Stan paid off some old bills instead. Now we have no product, no money, and no profits. If Stanley had bought materials like I told him to, I would have the money to pay you."

While John's explanation made business sense, I had a bad feeling in my gut. I should have said something, but I bit my tongue and bought his story. In reality, I believed his story because I needed to believe it. I needed to believe John. If I didn't, I was afraid I would not get my money back.

Obviously, Stanley, the CPA, did not know my rich dad's lessons. But it was not only Stanley who was in the dark. Most people do just what Stanley did. They work for money, then pay bills, and save what is left over. This is why most people live paycheck to paycheck. Entrepreneurs must know how to spend money to create more money—spending time and money on marketing, advertising, and sales promotions and offering sales incentives to sale representatives.

In times of crisis, for example, times when sales are low and income is low, most people tend to do what Stanley did—save money, or pay bills. This generally spells disaster. In a crisis, a time with low income or low sales, smart entrepreneurs know that they need to spend money on sales and marketing promotion, even if they have to borrow the money. When the sales start coming in, then they can pay bills and pay back the money they borrowed.

During the global financial crisis which began in 2007, most people are doing what Stanley did. They are cutting back, paying off debt, and trying to save money. This conservation of cash causes the economy to slow even faster. Businesses and individuals following Stanley's course of action may not recover when the rest of the economy does. They will be far behind the businesses that were spending and moving forward during bad times.

Story #2: History Repeated

When I asked how I could get my money back, John told me that the only way to get it back was to give him more money. Now you may think that I would have been smart enough not to fall for this line, but I did. Over the next three months, I raised over $50,000 from friends for John and his struggling business. As you may have already guessed, the money was gone as soon as I handed him the checks.

So how do you raise money? The answer is: You have to practice. In my Xerox sales training, I was taught to make 100 cold calls to get 10 leads. Out of those 10 leads, you get one sale.

To raise money for John, I wrote up a simple business plan, created a small promotional flyer, and began knocking on doors. Same sort of thing as with Xerox—I made cold calls until I reached my goal.

At the time, John's company was selling soap on a rope, shaped like a microphone, for people who like to sing in the shower. I found investors for his company.

Let me restate it: The ability to sell is an entrepreneur's most important skill. If you are not good in sales, then you must find a partner who is.

I was still working for Xerox when my friends began to call, asking for their money back, plus 20% interest. As my fear went up, as is the rule, my intelligence went down.

I was too naïve to know that it was stupid for me to be raising money and promoting products for a business that was mismanaged. I was unknowingly participating in a little Ponzi scheme, a smaller version of Bernie Madoff's billion-dollar scandal. Thankfully, I eventually paid back the money.

Slow and steady always wins the race. There are few grand slams in life, and promoting a business or an idea takes time.

Story #3: Come On Board

Again, like a fool, I asked John what I could do to help him get my money back. His brilliant idea was for me to join his company, make the money back, and help him save his company. And guess what? I took him up on his offer. So I worked hard at Xerox during the day and, after work, I crossed the street to John's office in downtown Honolulu to work on a plan to save his business.

Entrepreneurs need to work 24/7 during the start-up phase, often working for free for months and even years. It's the number of hours worked for free that defines entrepreneurs and separates them from employees.

The number of hours working or practicing for free also determines the level of success you will have in anything. For example, professional golfers invest years in study and practice before they get paid—*if* they get paid.

That is why it is best to keep your daytime job and build your business in your spare time. You may think otherwise, but you just might be working for free for a long time.

Story #4: A Desperate Glimmer

With all the money gone, John, Stanley, and I were desperate. This is where the idea for the nylon-and-Velcro surfer wallets came into being. Since we were surfers and sailors, we already used nylon wallets. We sewed the wallets ourselves out of old sails from yachts.

John thought these wallets would be hot sellers. He was certain nylon wallets were going to be the product that saved his company. Although I was not as certain as John, we began working on our business plan and soon we were the first in the nylon-wallet business.

The benefit of this whole experience was that I was learning to design, package, manufacture, and market a completely new product. The lesson was expensive but, in hindsight, priceless. Even though I would not want to relive any of it, this horrible experience is what led to the creation of my *CASHFLOW* board games, which continue to generate passive income today.

Story #5: Stress and Fear

John was wrong. The nylon-wallet business was not hot. We were now in more debt than before, and we were going broke faster.

Out of total desperation, I showed John and Stanley an idea for another new nylon product, this time a product I had designed. John and Stanley were surfers and sailors. I liked running. Runners had a problem: Where do they put their key, an ID card, and some money while they're running? Running shorts had no pockets and sticking all that stuff in your shoe or sock wasn't an option either. So I came up with an idea for a small mini-wallet that attached to the shoelaces of a runner's shoe.

Now completely broke with maxed-out credit cards, we launched our "Rippers Shoe Pocket" for runners at the New York sporting-goods show.

Believe it or not, that product became one of the "Hot New Products of the Year" in the sporting-goods industry. The Rippers Shoe Pocket even made news in *Runner's World*, *Playboy*, and *Gentlemen's Quarterly* magazines.

Entrepreneurs must learn how to handle stress and fear. Stress and fear must motivate entrepreneurs to become more creative, learn faster, and increase their knowledge about people and business.

In other words, entrepreneurs must be very fast learners and seekers of new knowledge, innovation and ideas. Fear is the entrepreneur's motivation to learn. If fear paralyzes you, keep your daytime job.

What this really means is that business grows only if the entrepreneur grows.

Story #6: Holding The Bag

Soon we were shipping wallets all over the world. Although we were internationally successful, our company was still going broke. We had much more cash flowing in, but even more cash was flowing out. In a last-ditch effort, John asked me to raise even more money, which I did. I still remember the day I walked into his office with a check for $100,000 from an investor. John and Stanley smiled and thanked me.

A few days later, I was in Chicago at a sporting-goods trade show, selling Ripper products. At the end of the show, I called Honolulu to report my results.

Jana, our receptionist, answered the phone. She was crying.

"What's wrong?" I asked.

"I hate to tell you this, but John and Stan closed the company today. They took what money was left, and I believe they left town. I don't know where they are."

If I did not have a heart attack then, I will never have a heart attack. The shock that went through my body was like being hit by a bolt of lightning. I felt like someone had kicked me in the guts. That phone call was the beginning of the descent to one of the lowest points in my life.

I returned to my hotel room on Chicago's Lake Shore Drive and stared out at Lake Michigan. Over and over again, I asked myself, "How could I have been so stupid?"

John and Stan were gone. Their debts were paid off. I was left holding the bag for nearly $1 million in loans, money I had raised from friends, family, and investors. I had no job, no business, no home, and no wife. She left me once the money was gone, when I sold our condo to pay off the credit cards so I could use them again.

I had hit the wall. I could not go any further. I could feel my life forces draining out of me as I asked myself, "How could I have been so stupid?" over and over and over again.

Rich dad had repeatedly warned me about doing business with John and Stanley. He often called them "clowns" or "con men." The problem was that I did not want to listen to him, so I ignored his words and warnings about John and Stanley. Rich dad said, "A con man can only con you when you want something for nothing."

Sitting alone in my small hotel room in Chicago, I began to let rich dad's words sink in. I began to ask myself, "What did I want for nothing?" If I could figure that out, I could find out why I had been conned.

I wish I could say I found a definitive answer. But so far, over the years, the answer I found for myself is, "I'm lazy. That's why I am conned."

A few examples of how laziness contributes to being conned include:

- Employees who believe in job security
- Voters who vote for politicians who promise to look out for the voters' best interests
- Investors who believe their financial planners' advice to invest for the long term in stocks, bonds, and mutual funds
- People who believe that getting good grades in school assures them of job security for life
- Desperate people who fall for pitches like, "Buy my book and become a millionaire overnight," or "Take this pill and lose 10 pounds without exercising"

- Anyone who believes the following statements to be true:
  - "We don't need money. We can live on love." (As long as you live with your parents.)
  - "I'm going to win the lottery." (Or get struck by lightning.)
  - "My husband and I have the highest of integrity." (This claim cost me millions.)
  - "Safe as money in the bank." (It must not be very safe then.)
  - "The government will solve the problem." (You're in trouble.)

I am sure you can add your own favorite con jobs to this list.

You Don't Know What You Don't Know

Although rich dad warned me about John and Stanley, he did not try to stop me. Instead, he would say, "Children do not know what 'hot' means until they touch the stove." So, he let me touch the stove.

His real lesson was: "You do not know what you do not know." Entrepreneurs learn quickly. He would say, "The moment a person quits his job and becomes an entrepreneur, what he does not know will immediately appear."

One reason why 9 out of 10 businesses fail in the first five years is because the entrepreneur becomes overwhelmed by what he does not know. It is what he does not know that destroys the business, even if he did well in school.

Con Men Are Great Teachers

Rich dad used to say, "The moment you begin your business, the con men and women will appear." He did not say con men or con women are bad. In his mind, con men and con women appear to do you a favor, to teach you lessons you need to learn. This is why he often said, "Con men are great teachers." He also added, "Just don't become one of them."

He taught me, "One of the most important jobs of entrepreneurs is to protect their employees from the real world." By this he meant that the world of business is one of the most hostile, vicious, and dangerous environments you can work in. One of the lessons I had to learn in my development as an entrepreneur was how to protect my employees from the real world.

I was anxious to learn this lesson. I had seen my own dad— who was an honest, hardworking, and well-educated teacher and administrator—become raw meat once he left the safety of the school system. He had run for lieutenant governor of the State of Hawaii as a Republican. He lost the election and became unemployed in his early fifties. Taking his life savings and retirement money, he purchased a famous ice cream franchise and lost everything. Simply put, he was safe as long as he worked for the school system, a system he had been in since the age of five. The moment he stepped outside the system in his early fifties into the real world of business, he was eaten alive. In less than a year, he lost everything he had worked for his entire life.

This is why emotional maturity and strength of character are essential in the world of entrepreneurship.

Murphy's Law

Most of us have heard of Murphy's Law: "Anything that can go wrong will go wrong." Most entrepreneurs fail because they simply do not know what they do not know, and they fail to fail fast enough to discover those things they need to know. In other words, success comes from failure, not from memorizing the right answers.

This is why so many so-called smart, well-educated people, like my dad, do not do well in business. They are smart in the world of the classroom, but are not smart in the world of business.

The Definition of Success Is Different

Success in the world of the classroom means not making mistakes. When your report card is perfect, you get an A+. The opposite is true in the world of business.

If you take a look at most MBA programs, the focus is on minimizing risk and not making mistakes. This is why so few MBAs become entrepreneurs. Most get their MBA with the hope of becoming highly paid employees. The same is true with law school and accounting graduates. They are trained and paid to not make mistakes.

To be successful in the world of entrepreneurs, especially in the early stages, a person must learn to fail, correct, learn, apply what was learned, and fail again. This is also the path to developing your Midas Touch.

This is why I started by listing my mistakes in the nylon-wallet business. This is why I respect Donald Trump. The first book of his I read was *The Art of the Deal*. The next book was *The Art of the Comeback*, an even more powerful book because he pointed out to the world his mistakes, what he learned, and how he came back. That showed me his strength of character.

Turning Bad Luck into Good Luck

Possibly the most important skill entrepreneurs can develop is the ability to turn bad luck into good luck. To do this requires emotional maturity and strength of character.

We all make mistakes. Mistakes are important because, when we fail, we have the opportunity to discover and develop our emotional maturity and improve our strength of character.

One of the reasons I believe John and Stanley failed to grow from a bad experience is because, instead of facing their troubles when times got tough, they lied, deceived, and ran. In other words, when times got tough, their true character appeared. When bad things happened, they turned bad luck into worse luck.

I'm not saying I put myself above them. I will never be on a short list for sainthood. Although I was raised in a great family, I did not always reflect my parents' high ethical and moral values. I was a good kid in high school, never drinking or doing drugs, but I could not wait until I left home. The moment I left, I did my best to do the exact opposite of what my mom and dad told me to do. A number of times I should have gone to jail.

In my process of becoming an entrepreneur, I had to return to my mom and dad's values, which meant I could no longer lie, cheat, or steal, especially when I was in trouble. Here are just a few opportunities that I seized to improve my emotional maturity and strength of character.

When I lost the investors' money, my rich dad encouraged me to go back to them and apologize. I then agreed to pay them back. It took almost six years to fulfill my commitment.

Rather than run from disaster, rich dad advised me to rebuild the company. With my brother Jon and my friend Dave, we sifted through the wreckage of Rippers and rebuilt the business. I learned more about business by facing my mistakes and rebuilding the company than I ever would have learned by running away.

I realized that I had to learn faster. Because I was lazy, I didn't do well in school. Today, although still a poor student and poor reader, I continually read books and articles about business and attend seminars. Here are a few of the things I have learned:

- *Inside every mistake is a gem of wisdom.*
  One of my best teachers, Dr. R. Buckminster Fuller, today considered one of the world's greatest geniuses, stated, "Mistakes are only sins when not admitted." Whenever I find myself upset about a mistake, I take responsibility for it, even though I would rather blame someone else. I then take the time to find the gem of wisdom in that mistake. Once I find the gem, the discovery gives me the energy to move forward.

- *Blame means to "be lame."*
  I often meet unsuccessful and unhappy entrepreneurs who continually blame others for their mistakes. They don't learn from their mistakes nor do they grow from the experience. What they fail to realize is that within those mistakes is the wisdom for a more positive future. Blaming is the worst sin of all.

- *Face your mistakes and admit to them.*
  Many people carry around their mistakes and regret having made them. Or they pretend they never make mistakes and then go on to repeat them. Others become criminals and lie about their mistakes. Again, they turn a bad experience into

something even worse. The fact is that if a person makes a mistake and lies, blames, justifies, or pretends they did not make a mistake, they recede. They do not advance. A good example was President Bill Clinton when he lied to the world about having sex with a White House intern. He could have been one of the greatest presidents but instead, he will be remembered for his lack of moral character, for cheating on his wife, and also for lying about it on television. It takes courage to face your mistakes and admit to them. It takes no courage to lie.

Mistakes Are the Gateway to Your Midas Touch

In school, making mistakes is bad. The students who make the fewest mistakes are called "smart." But in the world of business, making a mistake, admitting the mistake, and then learning how to turn that bad "luck" into good luck, is essential for success. Einstein stated that "only two things are infinite—the universe and human stupidity." However, I would add that a human being's ability to learn is also infinite.

As an entrepreneur, your mistakes may hurt your business, but so can your employees' mistakes. Often, if you attempt to correct employees and ask them to take responsibility and learn from their mistakes, they may leave, look for a new job, and let you be the one to pay for their mistakes. This is one reason why most entrepreneurs remain small with as few employees as possible. If an entrepreneur is a poor leader or lacks people skills, employees can be liabilities, not assets.

Making matters worse, employees can turn into criminals when the going gets tough, or when you turn your back, or when they believe that the money you have earned belongs to them. There are many crooks and con men in the business world. In the world of criminals, there are two basic types of crimes: violent crimes and white-collar crimes. Violent crimes generally involve a victim and a weapon or traumatic force. Most white-collar crimes are not prosecuted because lying, stealing, cheating, and incompetence, without a weapon or bodily harm, are tough to prove. In other words, biggest criminals you will meet are often honest, well-educated who lack emotional maturity and strength of character. They turn into criminals when things do not go their way.

In my life, I have not lost anything to violent crime. I have lost the most money to people who did well in school. They were smart people who believed they were the smartest people on earth and could never make a mistake, nor admit to making a mistake. This is not intelligence. This is arrogance, a tragic character flaw. An arrogant person cannot take feedback, learn, change or correct in a fast-changing world. They get left behind.

One of the most important lessons taught at military school is the ability to take feedback. On the first day of military school, feedback is truly in your face. It was amazing how many very smart young men cracked, cried, and quit simply because of this in-your-face pressure.

Entrepreneurs are always taking feedback, especially from their customers, bankers, workers, and sales force. Without straightforward feedback, entrepreneurs cannot make sound decisions.

If the entrepreneur is surrounded by "yes-people" or "butt-kissers," the business is in very big trouble.

The Mentor Difference

All public companies listed on the stock exchange are required to have a board of directors. So should you. Even if you have nothing but an idea, it is important to have good advisors. At minimum, you should have three advisors: a CPA, an attorney, and a mentor. Your mentor should be someone who is a successful entrepreneur in the business you plan on entering. For example, if you want to start a restaurant, talk to successful entrepreneurs who started their own restaurant and ask them to be your coach or mentor.

Both Donald and I had a coach and a mentor. We both had rich dads who were entrepreneurs.

Many new entrepreneurs make a big mistake by asking for advice from a successful employee, rather than from a successful entrepreneur. There is a world of difference between the two.

A Final Thought

Murphy's Law states: "Anything that can go wrong will go wrong." Combine that with the Peter Principle: "In a hierarchy, every employee tends to rise to his level of incompetence."

One of the reasons many businesses fail to grow is because the entrepreneur has reached his or her level of incompetence. In order for entrepreneurs to grow, they need to break through their level of incompetence, which means more education through more mistakes. It might take another 10,000 mistakes, as Edison stated when he was asked how it felt to fail so many times before inventing the light bulb.

I will use the metaphor of golf to better explain the Peter Principle. Let's say a golfer shoots a consistent 72. He or she is often called a "par golfer" or "scratch golfer." As most golfers know, there is a tremendous difference between a "par golfer" and a professional golfer, even though the difference is only a few strokes. Let's say pro golfers need to shoot a consistent 70 to survive on the pro tour. Any golfer knows there is a world of difference between a player who shoots a consistent 70, and a player who shoots a consistent 72.

That two-stroke difference is the Midas Touch.

If It Weren't for Bad Luck
Donald Trump

The fact that Robert ends with a reference to golf and explains the two-stroke difference as the Midas Touch is not only a great example but is one that's near to my heart. Most people know I'm passionate about golf—and golf-course development.

I am currently developing a golf-links course in Aberdeen, Scotland. I found this ideal location after visiting over 200 sites in Europe over a five-year period. I was patient because I wanted to find the perfect place, and I eventually did. The Trump International Golf Links Scotland is now in development, and the five years of site selection were followed by several more years of intense negotiation, particularly related to environmental concerns. I became almost an expert at geomorphology (the study of landform movements, which became something of a buzzword) due to the immense sand dunes on the oceanfront property. There was resistance from some people to my proposed development of this land, and great enthusiasm from others. It was the perfect recipe for a saga—so much so that a Scottish author wrote a book about the process I went through. He had enough material to fill hundreds of pages. (For those of you who are into golf or great stories, the book is titled *Chasing Paradise* by David Ewen, and the subtitle is "Donald Trump and the Battle for the World's Greatest Golf Course.")

I had to deal with business leaders, government supporters, and the locals. Even Sir Sean Connery got into the action by supporting me when I was facing a lot of opposition. Some people were sure I would ruin this land and not preserve it.

It became a story of international interest, which had its pros and cons. A popular American magazine had a cover story on one of the locals who didn't want to move from his house, which brought him fame and recognition as never before. His house, and whether he moved or not, wasn't of great consequence to our building project, but it became a great source of publicity for the owner as well as for the project itself.

The environmental statement for this land took up two five-inch-thick books. Everything in there had to be addressed, along with the business issues of the development. This site is of historical significance to Scotland, and it would be an expensive development for me at nearly one billion pounds (£). However, the construction project would create approximately 6,230 short-term jobs, and the development itself would support 1,440 long-term jobs.

Our research, both business and environmental, was extremely detailed. We worked with the Scottish National Heritage and spent countless hours working out every detail. To give you an idea of the scope of this project, Trump International Golf Links Scotland will include a golf academy, 950 condominiums, 500 houses, a 450-room hotel, 36 golf villas, and accommodations for 450 staff members. That's in addition to the golf links. It's an enormous development and there wasn't anything easy about getting it going.

While I was going through all this, I remained positive and knew that I had the tenacity that Robert speaks about regarding the Midas Touch. I knew I was in for some challenges—years of them—but I also knew that, with persistence, I would come out on top with a great golf course that enhanced the economy of the surrounding area without negatively impacting the environment. My passion was already there.
I really believed in the project. And thanks to the public encouragement of Sir Sean Connery, many people began to understand why the development would be in the best interests of Scotland's citizens.

During this time, I had many other interests to take care of, but never did it become a "back-burner" development. That's a key to good luck. Nothing should be relegated to the back burner if you want to excel on a big level. Everything is important.

Even though people may think I have great people doing all the work for me (and I do have great people), I stay very involved. I know every detail of this project. I took trips to Scotland repeatedly, not for pleasure, but to be on the job sites and to meet with our contractors, community officials, and the Scottish National Heritage. It was hardly leisure time. When it comes to this project, there's no overnight success story here. But every minute has been worth the effort.

Mistakes Are Made; Things Change

For those of you who are looking to be entrepreneurs or to grow your entrepreneurial business into something bigger and better that makes a greater impact, this is an important consideration. Every minute counts.

Here's my rule of thumb, no pun intended: If you can count the amount of time you put into a project on your fingers, then you haven't spent enough time on it. You will have to work on a project until you think you can't do it any longer. You will have to take a lot of criticism and negativism and hear "no" repeatedly. It will get worse before it gets better.

But if you remember the meaning of the thumb in *Midas Touch*— it stands for emotional maturity and strength of character—you'll reach your goal. It's a well-known fact that I experienced a financial turnaround of enormous proportions in the early 1990s. I never went bankrupt although a lot of people thought I did, but I owed billions of dollars. It was not a great situation to find myself in. It would be easy to see this as bad luck, but I didn't see it that way.

I knew the economy and real estate ran in cycles, but what happened in New York was devastating to many people. Real estate took a huge nose dive and the city hit some hard times, and those hard times included me. A lot of people were wiped out. My biggest mistake was that I lost my focus and was playing too much. I'd go to the fashion shows in Paris and didn't have a firm hold on my businesses. I just thought everything would keep rolling along with the money flowing in. My father once said that everything I touched turned to gold and I started to believe that. Things were easy and lucrative. It seemed that I didn't have to pay attention, so I didn't. I got a good wake-up call when things turned from onward and upward to onward and downward.

Fortunately, over time, I was able to regain my focus and my fortune. I actually became much more successful after my big loss. One of the reasons is that I had always seen myself as a lucky guy, and I still do. I didn't let the experience of a big loss change my view of who I am. I saw the whole thing as a "blip" and nothing more. I knew I had the skill set to get back into the game, just as a golfer knows and uses the same technique to get out of the sand trap and sink a birdie.

Do I still make mistakes? Yes, of course. But just as I did during my financial meltdown, I realize that I have no one to blame but myself. I take full responsibility because I am responsible for any situation I get into. As Robert points out, that's one gateway to the Midas Touch. Everyone makes mistakes, but it's what you do with them and what you learn from them that matters. And that's all part of emotional maturity and strength of character.

One of the greatest attributes you can have is an intense sense of responsibility. It is empowering, for one thing, and your effectiveness will increase tremendously when you own the good and the bad of all you do. In business and in life, this is an area you can work on. As soon as you take responsibility for all that you touch, the power is in your hands to make it extraordinary. For me, having that sense of control has been a catalyst for success.

My West Side Story

You may think that my success is because the Trump brand carries weight and makes everything easier, but I know that I am not always in control of our destiny as a brand and as an organization. There's timing to be considered. There have been many times when I have had to wait a long time, and very patiently, for projects to get off the ground, for things to happen. For example, believe it or not, I waited 20 years to see Trump Place on the Hudson River begin construction. How many of you would be patient enough and focused enough to wait that long? How many of you would have enough belief in the project to withstand the trials and tribulations it took during those 20 years? That's a long time, but my vision for the development was clear to me and I wanted it to be done. Was it easy? No. But once again, it was worth the wait, and it made me stronger and more resolute.

Here are some of the details. This story began in 1974 when I secured the option to buy the West Side rail yards from Penn Central

Railroad. New York City wasn't doing very well then, even though this was riverfront property and I was getting it at a low price.

At that time, I was busy with my other projects, including the Commodore/Hyatt renovation and Trump Tower. At the waterfront, I encountered great resistance from the West Side community which did not want Trump Place to happen. In addition, government subsidies, which helped make the project profitable, dropped for the sort of housing I was considering. That alone put me in a tough situation. Recognizing the deal just wasn't going to work, I gave up my original option in 1979, and the city sold the rail yards to someone else.

Fortunately for me, the buyers didn't have much experience in New York, and even less experience with rezoning. That's a complex facet of real estate in this city. Their inexperience caused them to make a lot of mistakes, and eventually they were forced to sell out. It was 1984 when they called to let me know they were interested in selling. I agreed to buy it for $100 million. That's about $1 million per acre for waterfront property in midtown Manhattan. It was a great deal. But I still wasn't even close to developing the property.

Between 1984 and 1996, my patience was truly tested and so was my tenacity. I had to deal with the antics of the city, which were plentiful as well as ridiculous. Business savvy comes with experience. Since I was much more experienced by this point, I used some of the city's disadvantages to my benefit.

Things still weren't great in New York, even by the early 1990s, but they were improving. For starters, because of the situation in the city, it was easier for me to get the required zoning. That helped because, as the economic climate began a turn for the better, I was starting to build at a good time. The timing was right. It wouldn't have been if I had not been patient and diligent. It's important to understand that this was the largest development ever approved by the New York City Planning Commission. It included 16 high-rises and uniquely designed residential buildings facing the Hudson River. We broke ground in 1996, and the results have been spectacular.

Trump Place has become a meeting place for the once blighted, but now-thriving West Side, with a 25-acre park that I donated to the city, bicycle paths for residents and city dwellers to use, picnic and sporting areas that bring people together, a pier, and open space for popular community events. It's been a win-win situation for everyone—the city, the residents, our company, and our brand. Tenacity definitely paid off.

Robert mentions the "wanna-be" entrepreneurs who may not realize how hard the going can get—especially when they're just getting going. I can relate to that. My first solo venture became so complicated that, at one point, I just wanted to forget about it. I'm glad I didn't, because it became my first major success and put me on the map as a developer in Manhattan.

The Grand Hyatt Hotel

Maybe you've heard of the Grand Hyatt Hotel in New York City. It's right near Grand Central Station. It's a beautiful hotel with four exterior walls of mirrors in a now beautiful and thriving area of midtown Manhattan. However, in the 1970s, that wasn't the case. This area had become dilapidated, and people avoided it unless they had to pass through Grand Central Station for their commute into and out of the city. There was an old hotel, The Commodore Hotel, next to the station. It was both in trouble and an eyesore. The whole area was depressing and becoming a magnet for crime.

I knew the neighborhood could use a big change, and I believed the first step would be to acquire and restore the Commodore Hotel. I remember that even my father couldn't believe I was serious about this. In fact, he said, "Buying the Commodore at a time when even the Chrysler Building is in bankruptcy is like fighting for a seat on the Titanic." We both knew it was a risk, but I was certain the renovation would change the neighborhood back into the flourishing area it could and should be. I could visualize it and, because of that, I knew I was right. That gave me a lot of confidence—which I was going to need.

About a year before I started negotiating for the hotel, the owner (Penn Central Railroad) had wasted about $2 million in renovations that made no positive improvement whatsoever. It was obvious that the hotel still needed a great deal more work, and the owner still owed $6 million in back taxes. They were ready to sell. I could therefore take an option to purchase the hotel for $10 million—but I would have to structure a complex deal on my own before making the purchase. I would need financing, a commitment from a hotel company, and a tax abatement from the City of New York. All of this was complicated, and negotiations took several years.

During these negotiations, I was looking for a talented designer who could make this old hotel into a spectacular landmark. I met a young architect named Der Scutt who understood my vision. I wanted to wrap the building in something shiny to give the whole area a new façade. I wasn't sure this deal would even happen, but I was so positive it could be great for the area that I spent the time to discuss it with Der Scutt and hired him to do some drawings, just in case, so we'd be ready.

I also knew I'd need a big hotel operator because a hotel with 1,400 rooms and 1.5 million square feet isn't a job for just anyone. When I reviewed the most experienced names in the business, the ones with the best track records, Hyatt seemed to be at the top of the list. I was hoping they might be interested because, although hard to believe today, at that time Hyatt had no hotel in New York City. I was right. They were interested. We made a deal as equal partners, and Hyatt agreed to manage the hotel after it was completed.

By now I had an architect, a hotel partner and rough cost estimates. What I didn't have was financing—and a multimillion-dollar tax abatement from the city. I was only 27 years old at the time, so it made sense to me to find an older real estate broker who had a lot of experience. Having someone mature would also help in the image department.

With everything proceeding on course after overcoming so many hurdles, we ran into another snag, a real snag of epic proportions that seemed insurmountable. Without financing, the city wouldn't consider a tax abatement, and without a tax abatement, the banks simply weren't interested in financing. We hit every obstacle possible, and I mean every obstacle. So we decided to appeal to the bankers' concern about the crumbling city around them. Perhaps they would feel guilty about not taking an active part in helping it become great again. That didn't work either.

After talking to what seemed like every banker in town with every appeal we could think of, eventually we found a bank that seemed to be interested. We spent countless hours working on the deal and it was looking good, very good. Suddenly, out of nowhere, someone changed his mind and came up with an issue that was of no consequence to the deal. That just plain killed the deal. We were astounded by the abrupt change of mind and came up with every argument possible, but to no avail. This guy just would not budge, and I'd had it. I remember turning to my broker and saying, "Let's just take this deal and shove it."

It's one of the few times I just wanted to give up. I was worn out. It was George Ross, my broker, my lawyer, and my occasional advisor on *The Apprentice*, who managed to convince me to keep going. He wisely pointed out how much time and effort I'd put into this project already, and he was absolutely right. "Why quit now?" he asked me. Because I'm not a quitter, I quickly resolved to stick it out. I also didn't want to be a "wanna-be" entrepreneur. This just happened to be the low point. You'll have a few of those too.

I came back from the low point even stronger. The low point became a turning point, and I was more determined than ever to get this project done. My new strategy was to explain the situation to the city, even without financing. The Hyatt Hotel organization was definitely interested in opening in New York. However, unless the city gave us a break on property taxes, the costs would be too high, and it would be impossible.

I made an effective point, and the city agreed to a deal that benefited everyone and made us partners. I would receive a property-tax abatement for 40 years, and I would buy the Commodore for $10 million, with $6 million going to the city for back taxes. I would then sell the hotel to the city for one dollar, and they would lease it back to me for 99 years.

If that sounds complicated, that's because it was complicated. But it worked out for everyone. Eventually, we got financing from two institutions, and the Grand Hyatt was a huge success. It opened in 1980 and marked the beginning of the revitalization of midtown and Grand Central. It remains a beautiful hotel to this day.

I think you'll agree that I ran into some bad luck while getting this project done, but I managed to work through the problems and things fell into line. As Robert mentions, sometimes we don't know how tough something is going to be. No matter what, if you want the Midas Touch, you'll stick with it and see it through. Sometimes I wish things were easy, but they usually aren't.

When I first became partners with NBC for the Miss Universe and Miss USA pageants, these pageants were not doing well. They were nowhere near prime-time material. They had very few sponsors, and viewership seemed to be lagging. Some people wondered why I'd be interested in them as a business (aside from the beautiful women). But I saw great potential and knew the pageants could become big draws if they were done well. The Miss USA Pageant 2011 took the top ratings for the evening. These are huge national and international events now and are considered the gold standard for beauty pageants. Some people say, "Well, you just got lucky," but it was more than that. We worked hard at making a good product by updating the format, hiring great producers and aiming for a high-quality product across the board. Our approach and focus served everyone well. Success is seldom a fluke. And the best part about success is that great feeling you get from taking something that was barely breathing and turning it into something alive.

There's a special challenge to turning things around, whether it's a neighborhood or a program or a building. Part of the Midas Touch is having the vision to see things as they could be, instead of how they are. Someone has to do it, and I've always had the energy and eye for improvement. It can be very clear to me, and I've never been one to avoid a challenge. I approach each project pragmatically and with emotional control, yet I maintain the enthusiasm necessary to get the job done. It's an important balance to achieve.

The Windy City

Trump International Hotel & Tower Chicago has won *Travel + Leisure* magazine's award for the number-one hotel in the United States and Canada. That was a wonderful accolade for a fantastic building. Once again, getting it built had its moments—and months—of difficulties. For example, three months after we began foundation construction, we discovered that water had leaked into the building site from the Chicago River. Since the foundation was being laid below the river level, the old river bulkhead that was already in place proved to be a concern. Would it hold? What compounded the problem was that the water was coming in through a corner where the bulkhead and the Wabash Avenue Bridge meet, which could be a very serious situation. We addressed that with painstaking care.

Next, we discovered a problem with the structural design of the building. We originally designed the first 14 floors and the base to be a structural steel frame that would have a reinforced concrete building above. Much later in the design process, due to China's industrial growth which absorbed so much of the world's steel supply, we encountered a huge spike in the world commodity price for steel.

It was back to the drawing board. We redesigned the building as all-concrete, saving several million dollars and also simplifying the construction logistics. This apparent setback worked to our benefit.

The timeline for this project underscores the patience required to get this building done. My plan for this building began in 2000, and we started construction in 2005. We had a few blips to deal with along the way but, if you have the opportunity to see this building, you will see that our efforts were worth it. Any "bad luck" was turned around to our advantage.

I consider myself very lucky from the beginning because of my family. My parents were great examples, my father was my mentor, and I had the benefit of a great education. I expect a lot from myself because I've been given many advantages. I've learned to turn around any bad luck I've encountered. That's why I know it's possible.

Getting It Done

Sometimes it's not my own bad luck that I deal with—it's someone else's. Sometimes understanding other people's problems is the key to finding opportunities. In 1980, New York City announced it would be renovating Wollman Skating Rink, an old ice skating rink in Central Park that had always been a popular attraction for kids, families, and people of all ages. After spending $12 million on renovations over a six-year period, the rink was still not open. So, in 1986, the city announced that it would start renovations again. Nothing had been accomplished. For six years I had watched this process (or fiasco) going on because I have a view of Wollman Rink from my apartment.

I decided to do something about it. Not having this beautiful rink available to citizens and visitors alike seemed like a waste. I wrote to the mayor at that time, Mayor Koch, and offered to construct a new rink and have it done in six months—at no cost to the city. I wanted to give it as a gift to the city and to the citizens.

My offer as well as my sincerity were spurned by the mayor, and he published my letter in New York newspapers as a joke. This tactic, however, worked against him when journalists and the public took my side. There was a great press reaction, and one paper announced, "The city has proved nothing except that it can't get the job done."

The following day, Mayor Ed Koch reversed himself and suddenly the city wanted me to take on the job. We had a meeting with city officials and agreed that I would put up the construction money and complete the rink in six months, which would be mid-December of 1986. When it opened, the city would reimburse me for my costs (if the rink worked), up to just less than $3 million. If I went over budget, I'd cover the overruns myself. I was excited to be able to do something about Wollman Rink.

This was an enormous undertaking. For one thing, the rink is over an acre in size, requiring 22 miles of pipes and two 35,000-pound refrigeration units. There was also water damage and holes in the roof of the skaters' house, and the work being done there had serious leadership problems. I knew I'd have to take an active part in seeing this through. I spoke to many experts and found the best skating-rink builder available. I checked on the progress myself every single day, both on the ground and from my apartment window.

A couple of months into the project, I had moments where I realized I could be hurting my reputation if this grand plan didn't work out, and certainly the media would be on it immediately. But I kept my vision intact for a finished and beautiful rink and realized what good luck it would be for everyone involved. The city and its citizens already had six years of bad luck, and I wanted that to change.

After five months of work, the rink opened a month ahead of schedule and under budget. I was relieved and very proud. The rink was beautiful, and the city was in a celebratory mood because it was back in operation in time for the holiday season. We had a gala opening celebration with Peggy Fleming, Dorothy Hamill, and Scott Hamilton, among others, to help commemorate the special day. Seeing Wollman Skating Rink open at last was a fantastic feeling, and all profits went to charity and the Parks Department. That's turning bad luck into good luck in a big way, for everyone. That's the Midas Touch.

Distilling It Down: Strength of Character

The stories we presented in this first chapter show that strength of character is fundamental to the Midas Touch. The thumb conveys that strength because it is the one finger that enables us to grasp and take control of things. It separates us from the rest of the animal kingdom, turning a paw into a hand. Symbolically, the thumb stands for an entrepreneur's ability to find strength when others want to run, hide, quit, or blame someone else for their failures. It also stands for the successful entrepreneur's unique ability to turn trying times into triumphs.

Most people would be entrepreneurs if winning were guaranteed. You've probably heard plenty of people wistfully say, "It sure would be nice to be your own boss." It sounds nice to be able to make your own hours and work the way you want to work. For others, the satisfaction of building a business and possibly attaining great wealth and fame is what makes the whole idea of entrepreneurship appealing. If it weren't for that darn fear of failure!

And that is the reason why most people don't become entrepreneurs. They simply fear failing more than they desire winning. Unfortunately, life has its ups and downs, which means that if you want to win, you have to accept losing too. Living life somewhere in the middle is impossible. Life throws punches at us whether we like it or not, and only expecting wins is unrealistic. What separates Midas Touch entrepreneurs from all others is that when they face a loss, they quickly stand back up, learn from their mistakes, and move on. Successful entrepreneurs know that learning from their mistakes affords them greater wisdom and strength for the next challenge. While failing turns many people into failures, failure makes Midas Touch entrepreneurs smarter.

The Classroom vs. Life

Here's the paradox: If "A" students are considered the smartest people of all, why don't they all become extremely wealthy entrepreneurs? The answer is because most "A" students are winners in the classroom where they win by making the fewest mistakes and failing the least. They learn that mistakes and failing are bad, so they do their best to excel. In the real world of entrepreneurship, by contrast, the people who make the most mistakes—and learn from those mistakes the fastest—are the winners. Business rewards people like that.

What this means is that traditional education programs either try to avoid challenges where we might make mistakes, or they approach such challenges with caution and hesitancy. That's not much better. Some people become paralyzed in such situations and can't make a decision one way or the other. It's no surprise then that most people spend their lives avoiding risk. These are the people who would rather have a steady paycheck and a job than great wealth and their own business. There's nothing wrong with that, if that is what you want.

On the other hand, entrepreneurs, many of whom are not the "A" students, love challenges. They know and accept that mistakes, frustrations, setbacks, and failures lie ahead. They know that the challenge of overcoming mistakes is their classroom and their pathway to becoming better entrepreneurs.

It's not that they want to fail. They don't. The difference is that, instead of avoiding challenges, entrepreneurs know that the mistakes they may make and the risks that lie ahead will force them to become smarter, better, and wealthier entrepreneurs.

Most business schools teach students to minimize risk. While most "A" students view risk as bad, most entrepreneurs view risk as a challenge. It's their opportunity to do what everyone else avoids doing. Risk stimulates their creativity and challenges their self-confidence. When they win, entrepreneurs gain a huge sense of accomplishment, which fuels their strength. When mistakes are made, and they will be, the entrepreneur's true character emerges and further growth takes place.

A Few Personal Questions

If you are wondering whether or not you possess the strength of character to become an entrepreneur, let alone a Midas Touch entrepreneur, you'll have to look inside yourself at your personal track record. Here are a few questions to get you started:

- How do you handle losing?
- How do you handle fear?
- Are you willing to work for years, without a paycheck, on a project that may never get off the ground?
- Have you ever been betrayed?
- How did you handle the betrayal?
- Are you trustworthy under pressure? Or do you stab people in the back when the chips are down?
- How do you feel when someone else makes mistakes that you have to pay for? Can you fire a friend or family member?
- Are you generous or greedy by nature?
- How do you feel when you're out of money?

- When you're out of money, do you:
  - Call mommy?
  - Call daddy?
  - Ask for a government handout?
  - Look for a job?
  - Go back to school?
  - Blame someone else for your financial problems?

If you don't know the answers to these questions or don't feel you can be objective about yourself, please ask a friend who will be blunt with you. You see, to be a successful entrepreneur you must be able to handle feedback. If you cannot handle blunt and direct feedback, it is better that you keep your daytime job. People without strong character cannot take direct feedback. Feedback is important because business is nothing but one giant feedback mechanism. No matter how great you are, your feedback will not always be great, and you'll have to be able to accept that. In the marketplace, if your customers do not like your product, they will not buy it. This is feedback. A company that has high expenses and low income is feedback. If you tell an employee to do something and they do the opposite, this is feedback. If you find a trusted partner stealing from you, this too is feedback. If your banker says no when you ask for a loan, that rejection is feedback.

Find a friend who will give it to you straight. As painful as it may be, get over it. Take the feedback, even if you do not like what they are saying. Think of it as a character-strengthening opportunity. You'll need as much of that as you can get. As we have said many times, feedback is easier and cheaper to take from a friend than it is from the marketplace.

You'll learn, through the course of reading this book, that becoming a successful entrepreneur is more than a great product, money, education, or a strong business plan. Being a great entrepreneur takes intelligence, but not the kind that we typically think of when we picture intelligent people.

There are seven different types of intelligences. Excel at one type in particular, and you'll have the foundation for the Midas Touch.

The Seven Intelligences

Howard Gardner, developmental psychologist and professor of cognition and education at Harvard Graduate School of Education, developed the theory that there is not just one kind of intelligence but seven different intelligences. One of them, in particular, is essential to the Midas Touch. Until you master this kind of intelligence, the Midas Touch will elude you.

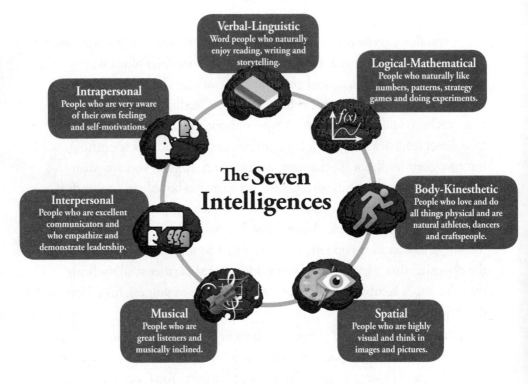

The Seven Intelligences according to Howard Gardner

Gardner believed that people have different kinds of intelligence with different ways to learn and process information. Whether you agree with him or not, we can all think of people who are gifted in one or more of these areas Gardner calls intelligences. We know people who are gifted musicians or athletes. We know people who are math wizards or amazing designers.

Among these seven is one that is crucial for success as an entrepreneur. You don't have to be born with it, but if you weren't, you must acquire it. Let's take a more engaging look at them all to get a lay of the entrepreneurial land. Can you guess which one is the most important indicator of entrepreneurial success?

Verbal-Linguistic

People who do well in school, the "A" students, are often gifted in verbal-linguistic intelligence. They are excellent readers and writers. They can quote famous writers and do well on essay exams. In business, students who do well linguistically may become lawyers.

Logical-Mathematical

These people love numbers and solving mathematical problems. They can give you the decimal equivalent of fractions faster than you can calculate it on your cell phone.

They are usually "A" students, and many of them go on to attain advanced degrees. Many remain in academia and become teachers, professors, and researchers. They may also work for universities, corporations, and government. Students who do well mathematically lean towards accounting, computer programming, or engineering.

Body-Kinesthetic

Most athletes are gifted with this intelligence. The most gifted and elite few may go on to become professional athletes or dancers. Some may lean towards the health or recreation businesses.

Spatial

Those with this intelligence tend to favor the arts, go on to art school, and some become very successful artists. People with spatial intelligence often become architects, interior designers, graphic artists, and website developers.

Musical

Students with this intelligence often dream of being a rock star or lead singer in a band. Some dream of playing with a symphony orchestra. They pick up instruments and gain familiarity quickly. They can hear music and almost magically know the notes they are hearing. People with this kind of intelligence are most happy when they are performing and will seek out careers in the musical performing arts.

Interpersonal

This intelligence is important for professional communicators, such as politicians, preachers, sales and advertising specialists. People with this talent are naturals at meeting and engaging new people, building relationships and winning friends. They are "people people."

Intrapersonal

While interpersonal intelligence is your ability to communicate with others, intrapersonal intelligence is your ability to communicate with yourself. People who possess this kind of intelligence have control of their own thoughts.

To elaborate on this a bit further, intrapersonal intelligence is often called emotional intelligence. It is your ability to control emotions such as fear, greed, anger, sadness, and love. For example, when you're afraid, do you react and run, or do you talk to yourself calmly, responding rather than reacting? When angry, do you control your temper or blow your top, saying things you later wish you had not said? These are examples of a person's intrapersonal intelligence.

Intrapersonal intelligence is also called the *success intelligence*, since it is required for success with all other intelligences. For example, a person could be a verbal-linguistic genius, but without intrapersonal or emotional intelligence, they may never study and will fail just like students who are weak in verbal-linguistic skills. Athletes gifted with body-kinesthetic intelligence may never attain professional status if they fail to practice and control their own self-talk.

The same goes for musical intelligence and all other intelligences. Have you ever heard a golf announcer say that a golfer "mastered the mental game"? What the announcer is saying is that the golfer has high intrapersonal intelligence. This is why it is often called the success intelligence.

In this book, intrapersonal intelligence is the thumb. It is the intelligence that gives entrepreneurs the advantage in the world of business. Intrapersonal intelligence empowers entrepreneurs to do what most people are afraid of doing, or do not want to do. You probably know people who did very well in school, but fail to do well in the real world. One reason may be because they are gifted linguistically and mathematically, but they lack the emotional control, the intrapersonal intelligence, to handle the challenges of the real world.

Most addictions—drug, food, sex, and smoking—are related to a diminished intrapersonal intelligence. In other words, it takes high intrapersonal intelligence to overcome addictions and bad habits.

Intrapersonal intelligence also plays a big role in delayed gratification. People with low intrapersonal intelligence have challenges with willpower. They want instant gratification so they go shopping when depressed, eat the cupcake when they're bored, take a drink when nervous, watch TV rather than study, quit when the going gets tough, lose their temper when they should bite their tongue, or blame others for their mistakes.

In case you haven't guessed it by now, intrapersonal intelligence, aka emotional intelligence or the success intelligence, is the most important intelligence for any entrepreneur.

Can You Develop Intrapersonal Intelligence?

The answer is yes, absolutely, but there is a catch-22. The catch is, it takes intrapersonal intelligence to develop intrapersonal intelligence. In other words, the more challenges you face as an entrepreneur and the better you handle those challenges, the stronger your intrapersonal intelligence becomes. The stronger your intrapersonal intelligence, the better an entrepreneur you will become. That is why becoming an entrepreneur is a lifetime personal-development educational process. Look at your thumb. Use it the next time you face a challenge to remember that what you are facing is your chance to gain strength of character and develop your Midas Touch.

Points to Remember | Things to Do

The thumb is all about strength, and it takes strength of character to be an entrepreneur. School smarts aren't the same as street smarts.

- There are seven types of intelligence. The one most needed by entrepreneurs is intrapersonal. When you have strong intrapersonal skills, you can control the self-talk that holds you back and undermines your success.

- Feedback happens whether you want it or not, so learn to take it and learn from it. Successful entrepreneurs welcome feedback and use it to their advantage.

- Being an entrepreneur is not a get-rich-quick scheme. Sacrifices are part of the journey. It takes strength of character to keep going.

- Being school smart isn't the same as being street smart. To be an entrepreneur, you need the strength and toughness that come from the street.

- Strength doesn't mean you must be arrogant, mean, obnoxious or overbearing. Strength is an attitude, a discipline, determination and drive. Find yours.

- The market hires and fires you every day. Midas Touch entrepreneurs get back up, brush themselves off, and go at it again.

CHAPTER TWO

THE INDEX FINGER
F.O.C.U.S.

"Concentrate all your thoughts upon the work at hand.
The sun's rays do not burn until brought to a focus."
– Alexander Graham Bell

Focus in Battle, in Business, in Life
Robert Kiyosaki

In June of 1971, I walked out to the flight line where my aircraft waited. This time there was something very different about that helicopter. It wasn't the same aircraft I had been training on for the past two years. On this day, my aircraft was fitted with rocket pods; four side-mounted, pilot-directed machine guns; and two machine guns for the door gunners. My real reason for training as a pilot was becoming all too real. My aircraft had changed, and that meant I had to change, too.

Until that day, I had flown with only one co-pilot and one crew chief, a total crew of three and no weaponry. Flying a helicopter with two pods of rockets, six machine guns, cans of ammunition and a crew of five is like flying a very different aircraft. Not only was it much heavier, which made it feel very different in flight, but the aircraft did not respond as quickly, which meant I had to be further ahead of the aircraft. I had to know what to do earlier, anticipate turning or pulling out of a dive earlier. Flying felt menacing. My helicopter was no longer a training aircraft. On that day, my helicopter gunship transitioned from a training vehicle to an instrument of war, and I knew I had to transition also.

A War Story

It had taken me two years of intense training at Naval Air Station, Pensacola, Florida, to become a pilot. In April of 1971, I was finally awarded Navy/Marine wings of gold. It was one of the proudest days of my life. After graduation, I drove across the country to California to begin advanced training at Camp Pendleton, a massive Marine Corps Base about 50 miles north of San Diego.

After graduation from flight school in Pensacola, most of my classmates were assigned to transport-helicopter transition squadrons. Transport pilots flew differently than gunship pilots like me. They flew much larger helicopters such as the tandem rotor CH-46 Sea Knight and the CH-53 Sea Stallion, which was often called the "Jolly Green Giant." Only a few of us were assigned to gunship school to fly Huey Guns and Huey Cobras.

The first pilots I encountered at Camp Pendleton had just returned from Vietnam. They were different from my training instructor pilots in Florida. Here, my gunship instructors were more serious, quieter, less polite, and less forgiving. Even though I was technically a qualified Marine Corps aviator, my new combat-veteran instructors treated me like I knew nothing. From April to June, I was tested and pushed to take risks performing maneuvers I swore should have been impossible. If a new pilot made the cut, they added guns and rockets and a new phase of advanced training would begin. If the pilots did not make the cut, they "flew a desk," which meant they were assigned an office job.

The movie *Top Gun* with Tom Cruise was filmed down the street from Camp Pendleton at Miramar Naval Air Station, also north of San Diego, although *Top Gun,* although too "Hollywood" at times, did depict the intensity of air-to-air combat training, an environment where being a good pilot is not good enough.

At Camp Pendleton, we were being trained for air-to-ground combat, which meant we were being trained to fly at extremely low altitudes. Rather than fight aircraft in the sky, we were training to fight men on the ground. I learned that the survival rate of gunship pilots in Vietnam was estimated to be 31 days and was declining as the enemy gained more experience and more modern equipment. Training got pretty serious, fast.

Wake-Up Call

The first day my aircraft was fitted with guns and rockets was my wake-up call. Up to that day, I had always been a "C" student. All the way from elementary school through high school, military school, and flight school, I was chronically average.

I know now that I was average because I was lazy and bored. But then I knew the school system graded on a bell curve and that in every class there are kids labeled smart, average, and stupid. There are a few smart kids on one end, a few stupid ones on the other, but the majority of the kids in the middle are average.

Happy to be in the middle, I rarely studied. I quickly figured out that, to stay in the middle, I had to do two things:

1. Know who was more stupid than I was. As long as there were some students below me, I knew I was safe.

2. Figure out what the teacher thought was important, memorize those points, and take the test.

In most cases, this method of study and observation kept me in the middle, a solid "C" student. I am not proud of my actions, but this is how I got through school without studying. In June of 1971, walking out to my aircraft now loaded with rockets and machine guns, my days as a "C" student came to an abrupt end. Being a "C" student would get me and my crew killed.

In January of 1972, a little more than six months later, I was stationed on board an aircraft carrier off the coast of Vietnam. A few weeks later, while on a mission north of Da Nang, the first rounds of enemy fire flew from a hilltop toward my aircraft. My crew chief, on his third tour in Vietnam, tapped me on my helmet, then grabbed my facemask, turned my head so he could speak to me face-to-face, and said, "Do you know what the bad thing about this job is?"

Shaking my head, I said, "No."

Without smiling, he shouted, "Only one of us is going home today. Either he goes home or we go home. But we aren't both going home."

Entrepreneur, Take Note

When entrepreneurs take the leap of faith and start their businesses, it is very similar to a gunship pilot putting on the guns and rockets and flying into combat. In combat as in entrepreneurship, being good is not good enough. That's one reason why 9 out of 10 businesses fail in the first five years. I would not be writing this book with Donald Trump if I had continued with my "C"-student attitude. First, I wouldn't be alive. Second, Donald does not tolerate "average."

I'm not saying you have to become a Marine and prepare for war to become an entrepreneur. I mentioned the transformation of my aircraft and the transformation in me simply because it is a real-life metaphor for the transition that employees must go through as they evolve into entrepreneurs. When people leave the world of job security, steady paychecks, benefits, and retirement plans, they too strap themselves into a different aircraft and prepare for a different world, a world where few survive and even fewer thrive.

Let's Focus on Focus

Aside from my laziness, I did not do well in school because I could not focus. If you look up the definition for ADD (Attention Deficit Disorder) in the dictionary, my picture should be there. I have the attention span of a cockroach sometimes. I simply cannot focus on subjects I am not interested in. School was boring and I hated being there. When the surf was up, I grabbed my surfboard and went surfing. At least the waves managed to hold my attention.

Transitioning from pilot to gunship pilot was good for me. I had to become a real student. I had to learn. I had to focus, not just for the sake of preserving my own life, but also for the lives and families of my crew. Just as surfing large waves forced me to focus, so did combat. In combat, there is no second best. In a strange way, war brought out the best in me. So does entrepreneurship.

Focus Is Power

Focus is a simple word, and, because of that simplicity, it is often abused, not respected. It's misunderstood. What most people miss is that focus is power. People who can focus have the ability to gather all their abilities and focus on the task or goal at hand. Focus is essential to success, and successful people are people who can focus.

We all know people who lack direction in life. They lack focus. We all know people who quit when the going gets tough. They allow little setbacks, such as running out of money, to stop them. Most people actually never start, allowing their fear of failure to stop them from taking even the first step.

We all know people who say they are going on a diet, but quit as soon as the chocolate cake is cut. The same goes for exercise. They exercise for a week, then quit and go drinking to relieve the pain in their muscles.

And we all know people who want to be rich, but let excuses such as "I don't have any money" stop them. And we all know people who would love to quit a job they hate, yet let the excuse, "I have bills to pay," keep them suffering eight hours a day. Health, wealth, and happiness are reflections of a person's ability to focus. It's the ability to focus their personal powers to achieve what they want in life.

Focus on Getting Yours

People can develop focus, and people can improve their focus. I'm living proof. Getting through flight school and becoming a pilot required focus. Becoming a gunship pilot required the kind of focus I didn't think I had. The ability to fly a powerful aircraft just above the jungle, and to concentrate on a machine gunner on the ground who was trying to kill us while we tried to kill him, required even more extreme focus. If my enemy's focus was greater than my focus, he went home. My crew and I did not. Today, I use the same power of focus in my businesses, in my diet, and when I go to the gym. If I say I am going to do something, it is my ability to focus that gets the job done.

We all focus on different things. That is what makes us different. Many people fail to do well as entrepreneurs simply because their life's primary focus is on security and safety. Many "A" students focus on achieving good grades simply because they want job security. Most employees want the certainty of set hours, set pay, set benefits, weekends off, and guaranteed retirement. The world of security brings out the best in them. The world of uncertainty brings out the best in others.

In January of 1973, I returned from the war. My year in Vietnam was up. I asked my dad for advice on what I should do next. He recommended that I go back to school, get my master's degree, possibly get my PhD, and then get a government job. In other words, his advice was to focus on job security and retirement security. I quickly said no to that, knowing my spirit would die in that environment. It would be like being trapped in school for the rest of my life and waiting for the school bell to ring. It had taken years and a war to get me past all of that.

When I shook my head at that idea, he then suggested I fly for the airlines, as many of my fellow Marine pilots were doing. He shook his head when I told him, "For me, Dad, that would be going backwards. I already know how to fly. I loved combat. I came alive in the environment of war. Flying for the airlines would be like returning home to drive a bus." I knew that was not for me either. My poor dad's focus was always on security. Once again, it was clear that his focus was not my focus.

In 2009, the movie *The Hurt Locker* won an Academy Award. In that movie, a young soldier returns from Iraq after being an EOD (Explosive Ordnance Demolition) technician, a person who neutralizes IEDs (Improvised Explosive Devices), one of the most hazardous jobs of the war. After being home for a few months in the so-called civilized world, the final scene of the movie shows him putting on his bomb-disposal suit and once again walking down a road back in Iraq.

When I returned to the civilized world, I too thought about returning to war, or becoming a mercenary fighting in Africa, or flying for the CIA in Asia. I couldn't shake the sense that the civilized world of job security would kill my spirit, and eventually me. That is why I became an entrepreneur.

Focus Defined

I like to think of the word FOCUS as Follow One Course Until Successful.

My favorite two words of that acronym are these: *until successful.* Focus, represented by the index finger, is essential in developing your Midas Touch, and the focus must be about bringing out the best in you.

Focus is also power *measured over time.* For example, it is easy for me to stay on my diet from breakfast to lunch. But to stay focused for years on the diet is the true power of focus. I have gone on diets, lost weight, gained it back, and had to lose the weight again. That is the lack of focus over time.

The same thing happens in the world of money. People get rich, and then lose it all. Lottery winners and sports stars are prime examples of the loss of focus over time. Many professional athletes spend years practicing hard to make the big money in professional sports, but are broke five years after retiring. They focused on sports, but not on their financial intelligence.

In the first chapter of this book on the power of the thumb, I wrote about a few of my many failures. If not for the power of focus, I would have quit. In other words, most entrepreneurs fail because they lack the strength of character, represented by the thumb, and the power of focus, the ability to stay on course until successful.

Focus also means staying successful *beyond the goal.* This means hanging on to the money after you make it, or keeping the weight off after you lose it.

As pilots, we had to stay focused on our target, even though the enemy was doing their best to shoot us down. Focus gave us the power to stay calm, think clearly, and act decisively. We never let go of our focus until the aircraft and crew were safe and sound back on board the aircraft carrier. It takes the same focus in business. Just because the business makes money does not mean the business is safe.

Success eludes millions of people simply because they lack the power of focus. When people are in a focused state, the words "I can't," "I'll try," "I'll do it tomorrow," and "maybe" get forced out of their vocabularies. In many ways, being focused means "do or die" and "for as long as it takes." When the going gets tough, many people lose focus and quit. They look for something easier to do. And worst of all, most people never start because they allow the words "I'll try" and "tomorrow" to dominate their thinking.

Have you noticed that people who lack the power of focus often lack direction too? They wander, going from one thing to another. To make matters worse, in the world of investing, many so-called financial experts recommend people diversify their investment portfolio rather than focus on high-performance assets. This is why many investor portfolios fail to deliver high returns or are wiped out in a market crash. Again, they lack focus.

Fact: Life Isn't Easy

Another reason why many people fail to succeed is because they focus on an erroneous belief that life is easy. Because of that, they always choose the easy road. They follow the advice that is easy, and they focus on small, easy goals. So they stay small. My rich dad often said, "Successful people focus on goals that are bigger than themselves. A person who has a $10 focus will next focus on $100. When they have $100, they then focus on $1,000. Focusing on bigger goals creates bigger people."

However, rich dad also warned against becoming a foolish dreamer. By this he meant that many people set foolish goals, goals that are far bigger than they are. I'm talking about people who have no sense of money at all and they dream of becoming a millionaire. No knowledge, no plan, but somehow it will miraculously happen. Rich dad said, "Dreams without education, plans, mentors, and actions create delusional people, also known as dreamers."

When I lost everything in my first business, my focus was on paying back the nearly $1 million that I owed investors. I focused on the smallest investors first, paid them back, then the next bigger investor, and so on. Those were the first few steps in our plan. It took years to climb out of that hole, but it was worth the trip because we grew smarter as we paid off bigger investors. From that, Kim and I created an audio CD and workbook, *How We Got Out of Bad Debt,* for those who want to follow our formula.

When Kim and I got married in 1986, we did not focus on becoming millionaires. While we had our *dream* of becoming millionaires, we focused first on $100 a month cash flow from investments. Once we had that, we focused on $1,000 a month, then $10,000, and so on. Those first few goals may sound small, the opposite of what I've been talking about. But when you are underwater by almost a million dollars, coming out with $100 positive every month was a very big goal for us.

The point is that Kim and I had our dreams, but we never lost our focus. And we kept increasing our goals as we grew. In other words, our focus caused us to grow. A lack of focus is for people who are comfortable, and either want to stay the same or grow smaller.

Focus Requires Education

When I knew Vietnam was my next stop, I became a true student for the first time in my life. I wanted to learn because I had to learn. Not only was my life on the line, but so were the lives of my crew. I feel the same way today as an entrepreneur. My most important job is to protect the jobs of my employees. When I fail to do that, which I have a number of times, a little bit of me dies.

I was a "C" student in school, rarely studying and always goofing off, but in business, I cannot afford to be a "C" student. I must constantly study, read books, attend seminars, and seek new ideas. Most importantly, I seek wise men and women, aka teachers.

At Camp Pendleton, I realized that not all instructors are the same. There are different types. At flight school in Florida, the instructors taught me to fly. At Camp Pendleton, the instructors taught me to kill or be killed. I had to go far beyond the simple skill of flying.

I carry that lesson from Camp Pendleton with me even today. I choose my teachers carefully. In high school, I had no choice over my teachers. If I got a bad teacher or a teacher I did not respect, I was in trouble. More than being a waste of time, a bad or incompetent teacher messed with my brain, my thoughts, and then my actions. Today, I don't let that happen. As an entrepreneur, I choose my teachers carefully, very carefully. I am extremely cautious of the people with whom I spend my time and to whom I listen.

Donald Trump is the kind of teacher I respect, want to learn from, and want to be more like. That's one of the reasons I enjoy spending time with him. Most of my teachers in school did not fit those qualifications. I'm not saying they were bad people. I simply did not want to be like them.

When I realized I was on my way to Vietnam—a place where the rule was "kill or be killed"—I knew why the Marine Corps instructors were combat veterans who practiced what they preached. They had been through the war, literally, and had come back to tell about it.

Looking back, I see my instructors at Pensacola in the same light as college professors. The first teaches people to be pilots, and the other teaches people to be employees. At Camp Pendleton, my instructors taught us to fight and kill—skills that went way beyond flying. That is why I now choose instructors who are survivors in the real world of entrepreneurship and investing.

Once you focus on your life's objectives, you need to focus on your instructors to make sure they are qualified to teach you what you want to know. They should have already been where you want to go and have lived to tell about it. Today, my company, The Rich Dad Company, makes sure our instructors, coaches, and mentors are successful in the real world of business. They have lived it and continue to live it.

A Final Thought

Becoming a gunship pilot taught me to focus and go beyond my doubts, fears, and limitations. The lessons I learned in combat I use today as an entrepreneur. It is not that I am fearless. I have a lot of fear, as much fear as anyone else. Courage is not the absence of fear. Courage is the ability to act effectively, in spite of fear. Courage is a spiritual power we all possess. It is the power over the fears that limit our lives. Focus combined with courage gives us the power to go beyond who we are, achieve what we say we will achieve and, in the process, become the person we want to become.

I have not met many graduates of MBA programs who have become great entrepreneurs. Donald is an exception. I've found that most graduates focus on job security, so most find jobs in big corporate organizations with a focus on becoming a CEO or CFO. If that is their focus of choice, getting an MBA was probably a good move.

You may already know that most of our great entrepreneurs do not hold MBAs, and many did not even graduate from college. A few greats are Bill Gates, founder of Microsoft; Steve Jobs, founder of Apple; Thomas Edison, founder of General Electric; Richard Branson, founder of Virgin; and Walt Disney, founder of Disney Studios and Disneyland.

Today, many colleges and universities have entrepreneurship programs. Very few people leave business school and become entrepreneurs like Donald Trump. This is because most instructors in colleges and universities are like my instructors at Pensacola, training future airline pilots to fly for big corporations, such as United Airlines or British Airways.

Camp Pendleton instructors took us green pilots beyond flying. They took us into battle and prepared us for the most hostile environment in the world. In my opinion, many entrepreneur programs in colleges and universities are lacking because the schools have hired "bus drivers" who are attempting to teach students to become "combat pilots". Both know how to "fly". The trouble is that only one of them has the kind of focus it takes to train entrepreneurs who can achieve the Midas Touch.

The Power of Focus

Donald Trump

Robert makes references to combat and military training. I attended military school and have some insight into what would be required to be a Marine Corps aviator. But his points are on target, whether you've served military time or not. Focus is of prime importance for both survival and success.

I remember a reporter who visited my offices at The Trump Organization, referring to it as "a day in the trenches with Donald Trump" because we worked so hard and so fast. I've sometimes likened business to being in a combat zone, because it can be. That means all your senses had better be on the alert, and your focus had better be one hundred percent.

I already mentioned that the reason I ran into huge financial problems in the early 1990s was because I'd lost my focus. Don't learn the hard way—like I did—how important focus is to your success. And there's a paradox involved in having focus. To be successful, your focus has to be broad enough to think big at the same time. You'll see how that works in this chapter.

Most people have heard of Trump Tower by now. It's one of the top tourist sites in New York City, and it's a great example of the power of focus. We opened in 1983, and getting to that point is quite a story. As is typical of everything I do, I was so intent on getting it just right that I would personally visit the quarry in Italy to find just the right slabs of Breccia Pernice, a rare and very beautiful, but very irregular, marble. I would mark off the slabs that I thought were the best with black tape. The rest would be sold to someone else.

Trump Tower Saga: Part I

That took place much later in the story, when Trump Tower was already under way. Getting it under way is another story. It took me close to three years to get a response from the man who controlled the land I wanted to buy. I didn't write just one letter or make one phone call over the years, but many of them. Later on, my tenacity would pay off, but it was a long three years. Robert mentions the "leap of faith" required for entrepreneurs. Mine wasn't so much a leap, as just plain holding on.

I wanted to build Trump Tower on the site adjacent to Tiffany's, and I had to convince Tiffany's to permit me to buy their air rights, their right to build a skyscraper on top of their store, for $5 million. That would also prevent anyone from tearing down Tiffany's and putting up a tower that could block my views.

Then there was the zoning variance I needed from the city. I had to know whether I'd have the air rights first, and the man in charge, Walter Hoving, was going on vacation for a month. He said he'd contact me when he returned. I could get a lot of work done in that month, but not without knowing if I had the air rights or not. Fortunately, Hoving liked my idea, gave me his word and said his word was good. It was.

Yet another New York City zoning regulation required any developer to have a minimum of 30 feet of open space behind any building. We'd have to cut the rear yard out of the building we'd designed unless we could get a small parcel of land adjacent to Tiffany's. This piece of property was owned by Leonard Kandell who had no interest in selling.

However, I found a clause in the paperwork for my Tiffany's deal that gave Tiffany's an option to buy the Kandell property within a certain time frame because it was adjacent to Tiffany's. I then went back to Hoving at Tiffany's to ask him if I could buy his option on Kandell's property as part of my deal with Tiffany's. Hoving agreed. However, Kandell said that since the option belonged to Tiffany's, it would not be transferable. He could have been right.

I realized I could possibly sue over this question, and there was a possibility of litigation that I explained to Kandell. Because neither of us wanted that, we managed a deal that worked for both of us. Kandell agreed to extend my lease from 20 years to 100 years. That gave me enough time to make it financeable and eliminate any prohibitions against rezoning. Both Hoving and Kandell were gentlemen, and I was fortunate to have dealt with them.

It actually took only half an hour to make the deal with Kandell. That part went smoothly. But you have to realize that it initially took three years to get a response to my letters of inquiry. During that time, I was building Trump Tower in my mind. I never once lost my focus on what I wanted to do. My plans were precise as well as vivid.

As I continued on my quest to put all the pieces together that were necessary to build Trump Tower, I was often reminded of Robert Moses, a famous figure in the history of New York City, and his comment: "You can't make an omelet without breaking eggs." I knew I had a few more eggs to contend with.

Trump Tower Saga: Part II

The property itself where I wanted to build Trump Tower was owned by Genesco. Bonwit Teller, the famous department store, was on it. It's fortunate for me that I'm a good negotiator because I needed a lot of experience in that department to get this deal done. Genesco and I kept our deal a secret for some time and had expected to sign contracts within a matter of months. That's when the news got out. Genesco was suddenly the attention of a great many interested buyers, including oil-rich, moneyed Arab investors. Equally suddenly, Genesco was trying to get out of the deal.

Remember all those letters I'd written for three years? They were going to a man at Genesco named Jack Hanigan, and fortunately I had received a one-page letter of intent from him. I let Genesco know that if they didn't honor our deal, I could and would litigate and could effectively hold up their sale of the Bonwit property. At this point, I wasn't sure the letter would be legally binding, but then again there was always the possibility I could become a big nuisance. It seemed things were hanging on a lot of "what if's" at this point.

Robert often mentions the risk factor in being an entrepreneur, and what happened next is a good example. I received a call from *The New York Times*. They'd heard about the deal with Genesco regarding the Bonwit building. Although we had kept this quiet, I knew it was time to make a move since Genesco seemed to be having second thoughts. I told the reporter that an agreement had been reached, that my plans were to build a tower on the Bonwit site, and that the store would be closed in a matter of months. I figured that would put some pressure on Genesco. Things had definitely escalated. The next morning the article appeared and, as soon as it did, all of Bonwit's employees went over to other high-end stores to look for new jobs. The result was that Bonwit's began to have trouble running their business. Five days later, I had the contract signed with Genesco. Like I've said before, business can be a lot like combat, and I wasn't fooling around. I was willing and ready to break a lot of eggs.

We had seen some pretty big battles already, and we hadn't even started the construction of Trump Tower yet! But sharing some of the back story gives an example of the kind of focus it takes and the battles that must be won just to get things going. As Robert said, life isn't easy, so focusing on the notion that life is easy will get you nowhere and just make you miserable.

Every entrepreneur, if they are seriously focused on what they are doing and want to achieve, will learn what it takes to win in the battle zone known as business. So be prepared to stick it out and take risks when you need to. When people look at Trump Tower today, they see the beauty, which pleases me. I see the beauty too, but I can certainly remember the war zone I went through to get it started. Once again, it was worth it.

Live from New York... It's Saturday Night!

Focus comes in different packages. So does risk. I remember when I hosted *Saturday Night Live* a few years back. I knew very well I wasn't a professional entertainer, but it sounded like great fun, certainly a new challenge, and most definitely a risk. Just like when I first considered doing *The Apprentice*, I knew being a new television personality could present some problems as well as advantages. I went for it anyway, and I went for *Saturday Night Live,* too. My focus was simply to do a good job and have fun. I'd definitely give it my best shot.

Agreeing to the show was one thing. What sunk in later was that this was a *live* show, without edits. If I was a disaster, I'd be a disaster in front of millions of people, without a second chance or a safety net. There were also many sketches to learn and perform, which meant my focus had to be one hundred percent, plus adrenalin. I was accustomed to delivering my own material as a public speaker, and *The Apprentice* is unscripted, so this was all new territory.

On the Tuesday before the scheduled Saturday night show, I met for an hour with Lorne Michaels' team of writers, led by Tina Fey. They asked questions, pitched concepts and were coming up with sketch ideas. By Thursday, we were reading through the sketches they had created. I could see that these people worked quickly and effectively.

They cast me in a variety of skits that included being a keyboard player, a hippie, a lawyer, a character in *The Prince and the Pauper* along with Darrell Hammond, and the spokesman for "Trump's House of Wings" with dancing and singing chickens. I wore a bright yellow polyester suit for that one. But the monologue, which sets the tone, came first, and the criteria for that is to be funny, like a stand-up comic. Everyone knows that isn't easy. What if I'm not funny? Now I'm thinking that I really got myself into something here. Plus, my focus was also on all those skit lines, a lot of costume changes, and many different sets and players.

On the Friday before the show, I went out on the set where all the stage hands and carpenters were busy working, and I said to them, "What am I doing here? I should be building, like you. I can relate to you guys." I really felt like I'd put myself in the trenches, and I'd better have a good game plan for what was going to happen on Saturday night.

What happens every Saturday is a marathon for everyone involved. We had rehearsals during the day, and in the early evening we ran through the show with a live audience of three hundred people, which was considered the dress rehearsal. It's also a way to decide which skits will make the cut and which ones won't. The skits most popular with the audience always make the cut. This meant I wouldn't know which skits would be in the live show, or their order, until about half an hour before the opening credits start rolling.

One of my favorite skits, where I played a romance novelist, was cut, and I found myself with five minutes to learn the lyrics to a new song that was a last-minute addition. But the real challenge was a brand new running order and pretty much zilch time to get ready for it. I know my adrenalin was running and, because of that, I had a strong sense of focus. It was down-to-the-wire time.

One thing that helped is that everyone at *Saturday Night Live,* from the writers to the crew, from the dressers to the performers, are all top-flight professionals. They were supportive and fun and always got me to where I needed to be for the entrances and exits on the set. When it finally came time to do the show, I felt excited. I turned the television on in my dressing room for a while to watch some golf and keep the big picture in mind. Things would go well, I was focused, and I wanted everyone to have a good time.

And that's what happened. I didn't even mind wearing the yellow polyester suit and performing with the singing and dancing chickens. In fact, that became a favorite skit, and the evening became a wonderful memory, as well as a great lesson. The power of focus definitely came into play for this one. And am I glad I took the risk? Absolutely. It proved the power of focus and gave me a great amount of respect for anyone and everyone who works on that show or on live television.

I think risk runs in my blood, or at least the quest for big challenges runs in my blood. Since I was a child, I knew I wanted to build skyscrapers. In fact, I built them with my building blocks, and I would borrow my little brother's building blocks to make my buildings even higher. The problem was that I would glue his blocks all together so he never got his building blocks back. Building skyscrapers was definitely a goal I had from an early age.

One building that is famous now, the Trump International Hotel & Tower New York, is a building that has won many accolades, including the coveted Mobil Five-Star Award. Its reputation as the number-one hotel in New York is well known, but few people know the history of this building. It's an interesting story and also represents a lesson in focus because it wasn't an easy ride. At one point, I came close to losing my bid on this building, and that was after a long and arduous process of trying to acquire it.

This building was formerly the Gulf and Western/Paramount Building. It was an office building at the time, owned by General Electric. When I took it over in 1995, it was one of the few tall towers on the West Side. It had been built in the early 1960s before zoning laws would prohibit a building of that size in that location.

I already knew this building had some problems, even before I bought it. One big one was that it tended to sway in the wind and would flex at the top, not just with high winds, but with winds of only 15 mph. On windy days, elevators would stop, and people who worked in the building would complain of feeling seasick. It's true that all buildings have some flexibility, but this was extreme. It was also full of asbestos, which is a known cancer-causing agent and would need to be removed. As if that were not enough, the outer curtain was made of glass and cheap aluminum.

When I heard that this building was for sale, I immediately called one of the owners, Dale Frey. You may be wondering why I would be interested in a building with so many major flaws. I was interested because the structure of the building was classic, and the building had very high ceilings. I also knew that if the building were demolished, it could only be rebuilt as a 19-story building with the current zoning laws instead of the towering 52 stories it currently was.

A lot of major developers were showing an interest in this building as well, so I asked for a meeting. I also started doing research to see what we could salvage. I put great people on the task who discovered that we could strengthen the steel structure. That meant we could keep the best features intact, like the high ceilings, which are perfect for a residential building. The location, perched right over Central Park at Columbus Circle, would make it a great location for a luxury residential building.

We had obviously done a lot of research, and General Electric seemed to have a very good reaction to everything I presented. However, I was in for a surprise when Dale Frey called to tell me they were putting the building's sale out to bid. They were asking the biggest real estate names in the country to participate and, despite my thorough presentation, I could be among them if I chose to be. I was starting completely over! I was dejected and angry, but what were my choices? I was definitely interested. So I got over the pride issue and went all out for it, again.

I took the extra time we now had to work on a tremendously detailed and well-researched presentation. I made sure we would comprehensively cover every question, every angle. If I thought we'd worked hard before, I was wrong. This time we went at it with everything we had, plus some. We took into account the profitability of the property as well as countless small details. (Remember the asbestos problem? That would need costly remediation.) While I knew I'd made a good first impression, I didn't count on any goodwill or brownie points. When Robert talks about combat and those who go back for more, I can relate. I went back for more and in a big way. My focus became even more fierce.

After my presentation, I can't recall exactly how long it took, but General Electric finally called me. This was a GE power group, which included Jack Welch, Dale Frey and John Myers. They'd decided to go with my proposal. I was elated. Focus paid off again.

According to our plan, only the steel structure would remain when we began to renovate the building. That was in 1995. Philip Johnson would be the architect along with Costas Kondylis & Associates so I knew the result would be elegant and contemporary. We also decided to make it a hotel-condo. A mixed-use building was an innovative concept at the time. I didn't think it was innovative as much as common sense. Since then, this format has been copied around the world. It has proven to be a tremendous success and is an example to all entrepreneurs of the advantage of using common sense. It can be a real time-saver and lead to new ideas that are well grounded.

This story is living proof that if you try once, you should try again. Keep that focus exactly where it should be—on winning. That's how the old Gulf and Western/Paramount Building became the number-one hotel in New York—the Trump International Hotel & Tower at 1 Central Park West.

I have a lot of golf courses now, but there is a special story that goes along with my Trump National Golf Club Los Angeles. It's pertinent to this chapter because it has to do with goals, focus, and vision. This golf course rivals Pebble Beach in its beauty, it fronts the Pacific Ocean, and it's truly spectacular. However, the problem it had when I bought it was also rather spectacular—the 18th hole had slid into the ocean, seriously damaging three adjacent holes. This 18-hole course had become a 15-hole course and needed some incredible rehabilitation. The owners had entered bankruptcy. I knew it would be a big job, but I wanted to make this course what it could be. I could see the potential and knew that, although I might be in for some lessons along the way, I couldn't just walk away from it.

I paid $27 million for the golf course, which included the land, the clubhouse and the golf course. An article covering the deal in *Fairways and Greens* magazine described the 18th hole as "Ground Zero plus $61 million" because that's how much it had cost to repair the damage caused by a landslide involving 17 acres of earth. On top of that, the water lines beneath the fairway had given way, causing even more havoc.

Rebuilding the course involved engineering a structural layer that would extend down the cliff to the beach, a series of walls made from Palos Verdes rock, and steel platforms every 10 feet as reinforcement. It was a complicated procedure, and $61 million was a lot for one hole. But I wanted it done and done right, which allowed me to override any doubts I had during this long and arduous process.

I also had a choice of whether to just fix the hole and keep the course as it was, and it was a nice course, or to redo it entirely and make it fantastic. As you may have guessed, I chose fantastic. That would cost me around $265 million (including the fallen-hole reconstruction), but I knew it would make the course as beautiful as it could and should be.

I wanted waterfalls, a driving range and crushed granite for the bunkers. One of the legends in golf-course design, Pete Dye, came in to do his magic. Everything was first-class, and everything was expensive. The best usually is, but it wouldn't be our brand otherwise. Trump National Golf Club Los Angeles is stunningly beautiful and has become a tremendous success. Why? Because that was my vision for it, and I kept that focus throughout the whole procedure.

Having a vision for something can be a very powerful force for accomplishment. Be sure yours is intact. Seeing yourself as victorious is a big first step and should stay with you every step of the way. Those who persevere, and those who take risks, have a real chance of acquiring the Midas Touch. Most importantly, never give up. And don't forget the learning curve. Learn something new every day. I do.

Distilling It Down: F.O.C.U.S.

The test for every entrepreneur is: Can you follow one course until successful? Even if the going gets tough, as it clearly has many times for the two of us, can you remain focused on the right things? Too many weak entrepreneurs will say, "This isn't working," and shift their focus to something else. They don't have the Midas Touch.

Leaders have vision, which is nothing more than the ability to see into the future. Entrepreneurs are different. They need more than vision. Entrepreneurs must have vision plus the power of focus. What we are saying is that entrepreneurs must be able to see the future and turn their vision into a profitable reality. You'll find that a lot of entrepreneurs, as many as 9 out of 10, fail even though they have great vision. The reason they fail is because they lack the power to turn what they see into a business that makes money. Look at the countless companies out there today creating free application software (aka apps). They can see the potential in their products, but they don't know how to turn their vision into a profitable business. Some will do the hard work and succeed, but most won't.

Our stories should force all entrepreneurs to ask themselves: How developed is my ability to F.O.C.U.S. (Follow One Course Until Successful)? Take a moment and do a quick self-assessment by asking yourself these questions:

- How long can you keep going when times are tough?
- How easily distracted are you?
- How well do you sell your ideas to others?
- Can you convince people to invest time and money into a mere vision, a thing that does not exist?
- What are some of the projects you have developed out of nothing?
- How prepared are you for the entrepreneur's world?
- Can you keep going, even when you doubt yourself?

Without focus, it's just about impossible to be successful at anything. Take golf. How many great amateur golfers do you know who can shoot in the low seventies or even high sixties once in a while? Not many, but you do probably know one or two. Most likely, these people have natural ability and are out on the course several times each week. But what separates them from the pros is focus. Successful pro golfers have so much focus that, when they get ready to drive the ball, they are able to mentally see its flight. When putting, pro golfers often see "the line" on the green between the ball and the hole, even though it exists only in their heads. The difference between amateur and professional golfers is the latter's ability to have the ball follow their visions of the ball in flight or rolling toward the hole. Entrepreneurs must develop that same power of focus in the game of business.

The index finger is closest to the thumb for a reason. The index finger needs the emotional strength of the thumb to maximize its power. The thumb gives entrepreneurs the strength to keep going. The index finger keeps entrepreneurs focused on achieving a vision. People who have vision, but who lack the strength of the thumb, only have vision. And vision without the strength of the thumb leads to dreams, delusions, and hallucinations. You probably know a few people like that, too.

Where is Your Focus?

School is ideal for teaching us how to enter the real world as employees. In fact, most kids go to school and are programmed by the system to focus on getting a job once they graduate from high school or college. This is why so many parents say to their kids, "Go to school to get a high-paying job." Or their teachers might say, "If you don't get good grades, you won't get a good job." We even hear and read it in the media. That's why so many people focus on becoming employees, such as nurses, police officers, and business executives. Some of the "A" students may focus on becoming highly paid professionals, such as doctors, lawyers, engineers, or accountants. The thought of another path doesn't even cross their minds because, unless their parents or other family members are entrepreneurs, few know the path even exists. They just don't think about it.

The CASHFLOW Quadrant refines and redefines people's focus:

Robert's poor dad was a schoolteacher who repeatedly reminded him to focus on getting a job with a good company (becoming an E or employee) or to focus on getting good grades so he could practice as a professional (becoming a highly paid S, which stands for self-employed or specialist).

Robert's rich dad advised him to focus on business ownership (B) and investing (I). Donald's dad encouraged him in much the same way and Donald never wanted to work for someone else. It wasn't even an option. His focus was on business (B) and investing (I) in a very big way, right from the start.

So what does all this mean? It means that it's no wonder that so many entrepreneurs fail. The answer is because they have been brought up and trained in school to become employees, or if they were deemed "smart," to become professionals. Think about it—most of us were brought up to be E's and S's. We were never prepared to be B's and I's.

Let's define E, S, B, and I in a bit more detail. You'll see why some of the quadrants make it tough to succeed as an entrepreneur, particularly a Midas Touch entrepreneur.

The E stands for EMPLOYEE. Employees can be anything from the janitor or receptionist of the organization to the division manager and CEO. Employees often are looking for "a safe, secure job with benefits." This is the definition of the "employee mindset." This mindset causes employees to focus on job security, steady paychecks, time off, benefits, and promotions.

Problem: It's difficult to become a focused entrepreneur if your mindset remains focused on steady paychecks and security. Given the lessons learned from the last recession and other economic downturns, how safe and secure are steady paychecks anyway? Or is it just an illusion?

The S stands for SELF-EMPLOYED, SMALL BUSINESS, SPECIALIST. When most people quit their jobs and start their own businesses, most move into the S quadrant. They have successfully changed their focus from a steady paycheck, security, and benefits (the focus of the E quadrant) to focusing on being their own boss and doing things their way. The mantra of most people in the S quadrant is, "If you want it done right, do it yourself."

Robert always says the S stands for "smart" which is why many doctors, lawyers, and accountants become typical high-income inhabitants of the S quadrant. Other typical professionals who live and work in the S quadrant are real estate brokers, business consultants, restaurateurs, beauty-shop owners, and most home-based businesses. One reason why many people in the E quadrant never move on to the S quadrant is because the S quadrant does not guarantee a steady paycheck or benefits.

Problem: In the S quadrant, when S's stop working, S's stop making money. E's get to enjoy days off with pay, sick pay, and paid vacations. Most S's don't have those luxuries, at least not at the start. Getting a business off the ground requires round-the-clock, day-in day-out focus. And there are no guarantees. Many new entrepreneurs go years without any time off. Another problem is that S's tend to pay the most taxes when compared to people in the other three quadrants. The people who give up the second highest percentage of their income to taxes are the E's.

The B stands for BUSINESS OWNER with over 500 employees. People in the B quadrant often pay the least in taxes, if they pay anything at all. Unlike S's who prefer to do the work themselves, B-quadrant entrepreneurs are looking for good people who can do the work for them. They look for others who are the best. They don't consider themselves as being the best. They look for people who can do what they cannot. They strive to use other people's talents and other people's time (OPT). Most of the time, B-quadrant entrepreneurs look for the best E's or S's they can find to operate their businesses.

Problem: Very, very few S's ever grow their business into the B quadrant because the B quadrant requires different skills and a significant change of focus. The shift is not easy but, when successfully done, a world of unlimited wealth opens up. Because of this lure of wealth, many people try to move directly from the E quadrant into the B and I quadrants, believing they can bypass the S quadrant. Both of us advise against such a giant leap. Although we both had rich dads who served as excellent mentors and role models, we still started small, gained experience, and gradually moved into the B and I quadrants. We tell aspiring entrepreneurs, "Keep your daytime jobs in the E quadrant, and start a part-time business in the S quadrant." We often are in favor of quality network-marketing organizations because the good ones offer sound business-skills training without much cost. These organizations also let you test and hone your interpersonal and intrapersonal intelligence—two of the most important keys to entrepreneurial success.

The I stands for INVESTOR. Many employees in the E quadrant have a retirement plan included in their benefit package. In the United States, the most popular plan is called the 401(k). Most self-employed in the S quadrant have an individual retirement account (IRA) or other retirement plan designed for small business owners. While participating in these retirement plans technically means E's and S's have investments, it does not make them investors, by Robert's definition. The investor skills it takes to develop your Midas Touch are dramatically different than the skills it takes to select and put money into a 401(k) or IRA. With those vehicles you are investing and presumably making money, using your own money. Midas Touch investing is making money using other people's money (OPM). That's the difference, and it is what separates the rich from the middle class. One reason why both of us started out buying smaller real estate properties was to practice using OPM—banker's money—to invest. Knowing how to borrow money to make more money and feeling comfortable with the process is critical to developing an entrepreneur's Midas Touch in the B and I quadrants. Through practice, mistakes, and lessons learned, we have gained the skills to raise money. We know how to find deals that people want to invest in, and have even taken companies public. We have used OPM to make money for ourselves and others. This ability is a dream of many entrepreneurs.

Problem: Unfortunately, entrepreneurs who build a business in the S quadrant find it difficult to raise capital. They often don't speak the language but, even if they do, true I-quadrant investors do not invest in S-quadrant businesses unless the S-quadrant business is ready to expand into the B quadrant. Then, I-quadrant investors love to lend money or become equity partners. But if an S-business isn't ready, which is most often the case, the entrepreneur has no other choice than to borrow money from friends, family, and the Small Business Administration (SBA). Their ability to really grow is severely limited.

In contrast, where do you think the investment managers of 401(k) and IRA plans invest the billions they bring in through the retirement plans of the E's and S's? You guessed it. They invest in the businesses and the projects of the B's and I's. In other words, E's and S's save money in the bank or with an investment company. B's and I's borrow the money from the E's and S's via the banks and investment companies to make themselves richer. The same is true with traditional pension funds. Pension funds of the E's finance many projects for the B's and I's.

Once you understand the implications behind the CASHFLOW Quadrant, it's easy to see why making the leap to the B and I quadrants is something every entrepreneur should aspire to. It is the opposite of what we are taught to believe in school.

Focus on Capitalism

America prides itself on being a capitalist economy. The model has served our country well for a long time. When you focus on the skills of the B and I quadrants, you are focusing on gaining the skills of a capitalist. True capitalists do not work for money. They focus instead on using OPT and OPM to make more money. By using OPT and OPM, the tax laws give capitalists tax breaks while taxing the E's and S's. This means that the harder the E and S work for money, the more taxes they pay. The more the B and I use OPT and OPM to make money, the less taxes they pay. This is not a loophole. It is the way our government incentivizes people to create businesses that create jobs.

You might be thinking, "Wait a minute. I know some pretty high-paid employees, and that plastic surgeon down the street is rolling in the dough." You'd be right. It is absolutely possible for E's and

S's to make a lot of money in their respective quadrants. But, as we clearly demonstrate, the big bucks, the real magic, the true alchemy of capitalism is created by entrepreneurs who focus on developing their skills in the B and I quadrants. When you think of the real alchemists of capitalism—individuals such as Steve Jobs, Bill Gates, Richard Branson, Sergey Brin, and Mark Zuckerberg—most created their fame and fortune from the B and I quadrants. They created monster businesses in the B quadrant, and the I quadrant showered them with wealth for their efforts.

Is Your Focus Too Narrow?

The more time you spend in school, the narrower your focus becomes because the more you know about a particular subject, the more specialized you become. Consider this: You graduate from high school, then college, and then graduate school. With each degree, you become more and more specialized. If you're good in math, you may go on to become an accountant. If you excel in reading and writing, you may go on to law school to become a lawyer, or journalism school to become a reporter or blogger. And if you happen to be a science whiz, you may choose medical school, which then means further training in a specialty that, when everything is added up, can take a decade or more. If you have an interest in business, it's natural to think that in today's world, an MBA is a must for any level of success.

By the time you earn that JD or MD or PhD, you are among the people in the world who know the most about the least. You are a specialist, rather than a generalist.

We both live and breathe the opposite. We know something about a lot of things and can operate successfully in many worlds. We have the wisdom of a generalist, rather than the deep knowledge of the specialist.

Are You Missing the Big Picture?

The reason we bring this generalist-specialist concept to light is because, when you are overly specialized, it is very easy to miss the big picture of business. When people take their intense specialization and combine it with their programming from school to "get a good job," it's no wonder the whole concept of building a business or becoming an investor isn't even on the radar for most people. They are too busy living and working as E's and S's to ever conceive that B's and I's exist. They miss the big picture. If this describes you, take heart. You are like most people, but at least you are now entering into enlightenment.

How This Applies to Entrepreneurs

What we are saying through our own experiences is that Midas Touch entrepreneurs are generalists who find and hire the best possible specialists to do the work. As generalists, they then help make the business and the specialists successful.

The B-I Triangle illustrates the 8 Integrities of Business, with each element being an integrity. Midas Touch entrepreneurs, the generalists, must work on the perimeter of the triangle. They hire specialists to work inside the triangle.

We're talking about the person who, for example, has an outstanding recipe for chocolate chip cookies. Everyone loves them and people are always asking to buy them, so the baker goes into business. She's excellent at baking the cookies, but when it comes to accounting, sales, marketing, legal issues—important aspects of any business—she is ill-equipped and no longer enjoys her work. She wants to bake cookies. Now, all of a sudden, she's no longer a baker. She's a bookkeeper, lawyer, and marketer, and not doing well at any of them. The same thing can happen to an accountant who goes into business and finds out he has to be a marketer and sales rep too. Or the lawyer who focuses too heavily on the legal aspects of the business and prevents his own success. You get the point here. It is next to impossible to "do it all" well, regardless of how smart you are or the excellent grades you got in school. So, businesses fail.

Both of us learned how to live and work on the perimeter of the triangle by attending military schools. That's where we learned leadership. This training is perfectly suited to entrepreneurship, where the main job of the entrepreneur is to define the mission, find and inspire the team, and lead. If military school teaches us to work on the outside integrities, traditional school teaches us how to live and work on the inside integrities.

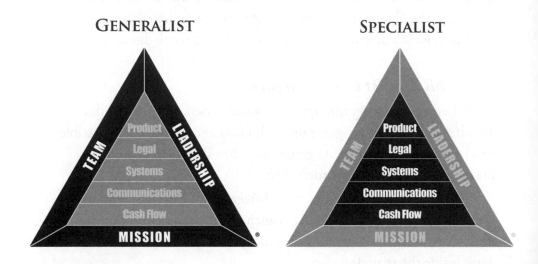

This diagram defines even more clearly why nine out of 10 businesses fail. It's because the E's and S's who are migrating to the B and I quadrants become overwhelmed by the 8 integrities.

We're talking about the person who, for example, has an amazing recipe for chocolate chip cookies. Everyone loves them and people are always asking to buy them, so the baker goes into business. She's excellent at baking the cookies, but when it comes to accounting, sales, marketing, legal issues—important aspects of any business—she is ill-equipped and no longer enjoys her work. She wants to bake cookies. Now all of a sudden, she's no longer a baker. She's a bookkeeper, lawyer and marketer and doing none of them well. The same thing can happen to an accountant who goes into business and finds out he has to be a marketer and sales rep too. Or the lawyer who focuses too heavily on the legal aspects of the business and prevents his own success. You get the point here. It is next to impossible to "do it all" well, regardless of how smart you are or the excellent grades you got in school. So, businesses fail.

We learned how to live and work on the perimeter of the triangle from attending military school. That's where we learned leadership. This training is perfectly suited to entrepreneurship where the main job of the entrepreneur is to define the mission, find and inspire the team, and lead. If military school teaches us to work on the outside integrities, traditional school teaches us how to live and work on the inside integrities.

MILITARY SCHOOL   TRADITIONAL SCHOOL

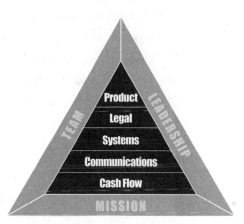

Three Elements That Give Business Its Structure

So what exactly are the skills that we learned in military school? The following experience-based definitions will give some insight. Let's break them down:

Mission

This is the spiritual reason for the existence of the business. In military school, the first thing they teach you is the importance of mission. It makes sense when you think about it. In religion, missionaries have a mission and focus on it. Too many corporations don't recognize the importance of mission. They create mission statements that are flat and uninspiring. They totally miss this massive opportunity to define the spiritual purpose of the business.

Team

Some think that military school teaches people how to be followers, how to conform, and how to respond to commands. Both of us understand that the ability to follow orders is the ability to focus. When everyone learns how to focus, you have the foundations of an excellent team. In military school, teamwork is not just a subject. It is a way of life, practiced every minute of every day.

By contrast, traditional schools are not about teamwork at all. Maybe there is an element of teamwork in school sports, but certainly not in the classroom where everyone is competing for grades. It's every student for themselves. It is a system of winners and losers, with the "A" students, and to some extent the "B" students, beating up on the "C," "D," and "F" students. Even if there are study groups where students can cooperate and learn together, when it's test time, the team is dissolved and it's back to competition. "Cooperate" on a test and you are labeled a cheater!

When it comes to teams in the military, cooperation is essential for survival. In business, cooperation is essential to success. We can't achieve much of anything on our own in this world, and that includes survival or success. So ironically, rather than foster cooperation, schools foster competition. Employees enter the workforce with a competitive, rather than a team-based, mindset. They compete for promotions, higher pay, bigger offices, more prestigious titles, you name it. One of the biggest challenges an entrepreneur faces is to break employees of their competitive, win/lose mentality and replace it with a team mentality. Mission goes a long way to make that happen. So does strong leadership.

Leadership

In military school, we developed our leadership skills by taking and giving orders. In that world, it was a way of life. Anyone who couldn't take or give orders was soon washed out. It was an environment of discipline, and there were no exceptions.

Perhaps you've heard the saying, "There is no such thing as bad soldiers. There are only bad leaders." That philosophy is drummed into the head of every future military officer. The same holds true in business. There are no bad employees, only bad leaders.

Think about companies you've worked for. If a business is financially struggling with low morale, declining productivity, dropping sales, and increasing expenses, it is due to poor leadership. Leaders, true leaders, take responsibility for the success of the team and understand that they must also take responsibility for the failure. Too often entrepreneurs blame a lack of performance on employees, the economy, or competitors. However, the best entrepreneurs look at themselves first to uncover their own mistakes and learn from them.

So are we saying you need to quit your job, shut down your business, and go to military school to learn leadership? No. You can learn leadership, team-building, and mission-inspiring skills from many places in life. We already mentioned sports. Becoming the captain of a team in your community softball or basketball league will build these skills in you. So will chairing a church committee, serving on the board of a professional organization, or being in charge of an event for a favorite charity. Putting yourself in leadership positions will give you the skills you need and help you network, which is always good for business.

Both of us recommend a part-time network-marketing business as another means of gaining leadership training. These opportunities force you to meet and communicate with people. This is a tough thing for many people, but is an absolute requirement for a successful entrepreneur. It's better to stretch when the stakes are low than to do it when your life depends on it. You may find out that this entrepreneurship thing isn't for you, and that's okay. People skills are not optional. They absolutely are required to become a successful B or I.

The reason why learning to take orders is so critical to leadership is because, before becoming a good leader, you must learn how to be a good follower. Only then can you communicate effectively with the people you want to follow you. Many very smart S's fail to become B's or I's because they can't communicate well with people. They don't make friends or build relationships well. They may be able to manage 10 to 20 people just like themselves, but they cannot handle larger groups of people with different skill sets and different backgrounds. They may be good one-on-one, but they are weak one to 100, one to 1,000, or one to 1 million. Thanks to our leadership training, both of us have influenced millions of people throughout the world.

Five Elements of Business Operation

The outer three integrities on the B-I Triangle's perimeter give power to the interior five integrities which are generally taught by traditional education. When even one of the three integrities of mission, team, and leadership is weak, the interior five integrities cannot possibly hold their shape. Problems inevitably occur, and businesses either stall, falter, or outright fail. When a business is having trouble, look at this triangle. In nearly every case, you will be able to pinpoint the source of the problem within one or more of these 8 integrities. Let's look in detail at the other five:

Product

Most new entrepreneurs say, "I have a great idea for a new product." As you can see from the B-I Triangle diagram, product takes up the smallest area of the triangle. While the product is important, it is the least important integrity. You might be surprised at that, but think about this. The world is filled with great products, many of which never make it to market or, when they do, die a quick death. The world does not lack great product ideas—you've probably had many of them yourself. What the world lacks are great entrepreneurs who can bring great products to life.

Most new entrepreneurs focus only on the product. They spend all their time honing their ideas and may even contract with companies that promise to advise them and develop prototypes. It takes a lot of money and a lot of time. In the end, the prototypes usually end up, not in stores, but tucked away in boxes, forgotten. A great entrepreneur knows how to turn a product idea into a great product by focusing on building a great B-I Triangle. The B-I Triangle isn't just a concept. It is a tool that many successful entrepreneurs have modeled their companies around.

Again, notice the importance of the word "focus" and what people focus on.

Legal

Robert learned early that a product without legal protection is everyone's product, not yours. His Velcro-wallet idea was copied over and over. Legal agreements are important because they create property. In the case of the wallet business, legal agreements would have created *intellectual* property. In the case of Donald's world of real estate, legal agreements define *real* property ownership, rights and limitations.

In business, you can't operate without legal agreements, which are essential to defining and creating products. Through patents, trademarks, licenses, and service agreements for services, a company builds its own property, which adds value and protection to the company. Without a strong legal team and sound legal agreements, you will always have confusion, chaos, even crime— all of which costs money and weakens the business.

Systems

A business is a system of systems. It has to be, or no business would ever grow beyond the capabilities of its founder and maybe a few key people. The bigger it gets without systems in place, the more fragile it becomes. Our physical bodies, and even a car, are both systems of systems. Our bodies are made up of systems like the skeletal system, the nervous system, the digestive system, and the endocrine system. A car has a brake system, fuel system, electrical system, exhaust system, and so on. They all have a specific function, and ideally they all work together.

In a business, you'll have accounting systems, communication systems, legal systems, supply-chain systems, manufacturing systems, distribution systems, and many others. The point is that the whole business, body, or car relies on its systems to operate effectively. It only takes one system falter or failure to hinder or shut down the entire body, car, or business. Imagine what it would be like to be driving along and have a brake failure. Think about what it is like for a two-pack-a-day smoker to run a mile. Imagine trying to grow a business run by accountants who refuse to spend money on advertising in an attempt to save money. In all these cases, one system failure or falter can be disastrous.

Communications

Entrepreneurs must be great communicators and speak many languages—and we are not talking necessarily about French, Spanish, German, or Mandarin. We are talking about the languages of business. Entrepreneurs must be able to speak the language of the law. They must be able to talk accounting, real estate, marketing, Internet, and every other discipline within their companies. Entrepreneurs must also understand and learn to speak the language of their customers. Only that way can leaders carry on meaningful conversations and make solid decisions.

Have you ever worked for a company where the leader was just "out of it" and didn't have a clue about anything you were doing? That's an example of a leader who did not take the time to learn the language of your specialty. That's a big mistake in business.

Learning the languages of business is no different than learning a foreign language. It takes time and practice. And just as the best way to learn a foreign language is to travel abroad and immerse yourself in the culture, the same goes for learning the languages of business. Just dive in and begin experiencing and hearing and then speaking the language. As leaders, entrepreneurs must encourage their team to foster communication and understanding, both inside and outside the business.

Cash Flow

Often this is called "the bottom line" and appropriately, it is at the bottom of the triangle. Cash flow is similar to blood flow in a body or fuel flow through a car. Without cash, blood, or fuel flowing, the business, body, and car stop operating. A body can hemorrhage blood, a car can have a fuel leak, and a business can hemorrhage cash. As if the entrepreneur doesn't have enough to do as leader, another role is to make sure enough cash is flowing to all 8 integrities (aka expenses) and still keep the company profitable.

You can see why, with all these high-level roles, it is impossible for Midas Touch entrepreneurs who want to grow their companies to get mired in any one of these five interior integrities. Even though they may be more comfortable working in their specialty, they must act as a leader and work to get all the specialists in the five interior integrities to work together. So many highly educated people fail to recognize this and fail as entrepreneurs, or never reach their true potential. They fail to speak all 8 languages and believe that the one specialty they are best at is the most important. They fail to see that all 8 integrities must work together. They are all essential to the growth and profitability of the business.

In case you're wondering why these are called the "8 Integrities" and not the "8 Areas" or "8 Specialties" or some other word, here is your answer. The word "integrity," by definition, means "whole and complete." An entrepreneur must focus on the whole business, the 8 integrities, not just their specialty.

How to Prepare

Being an entrepreneur is a big task. It is not easy. So what can you do to prepare?

First and foremost, expand your focus. In the example earlier in this chapter, if you want to have a cookie company, you're going to have to expand your focus beyond baking cookies. Most entrepreneurs focus too narrowly. Dive into your business, and business in general, to study and learn the language of the 8 Integrities of Business. In the process, you'll learn business in the real world, which is the best way.

We also recommend that you gain experience before starting your own business. With your new-found awareness of the 8 Integrities, get a job in the E quadrant and observe the B-I Triangle in action. You'll learn as much or more from a company that is doing it wrong, as you will from one that is doing it right.

This may sound crazy, but flipping burgers at McDonald's is one of the best jobs you can have for observing the B-I Triangle. This company is a master of the 8 Integrities of Business. McDonald's has the very best business systems in the world. Whether you join the McDonald's team or work at another business, take the B-I Triangle to work and begin to notice how all 8 integrities operate in unison. When a problem arises in the business, use the B-I Triangle as a guide and troubleshoot the integrities that are not working. One year of this, even part-time, will give you a significant head start over an entrepreneur who only has a dream, but no real-life experience. Remember, you are not looking for a career. You are looking for the best training ground. Don't work to earn. Work to learn.

Even if you do not work for McDonald's, go to one of their restaurants, order a Big Mac with a drink and fries, and notice how long it takes for the food to arrive and your money to change hands. Then sit down and, as you are eating your meal, think about everything that went into getting you into that restaurant and everything that went into delivering the product. If you can build a business of any sort that operates with such high efficiency—sourcing goods like meat, buns, fries, drinks, napkins, straws, and more from all over the world, and then pulling it all together so that the average high-school-educated employee can be successful—you will have developed your Midas Touch. You'll have made it to the B quadrant, a task few entrepreneurs ever achieve.

Which Quadrant Is Best For You?

You can find your Midas Touch in any of the quadrants. Many employees climb the corporate ladder to great success and self-satisfaction. The same is true in the S quadrant. Many professionals have developed very lucrative law practices, medical practices, consultancies, and small businesses. Your job is to now focus on which quadrant is best for you. Which one will allow you to fulfill your dreams? If you are attracted to the B and I quadrants, then both of us have programs for you. Donald already has the mega-hit *The Apprentice*. It's a crash course on the B-I Triangle and, if you win on that program, you have an opportunity to work for one of the greatest entrepreneurs of all time.

Robert's organization, The Rich Dad Company, is in the process of developing an ambitious program called GEO, which stands for Global Entrepreneurs Organization. It will be a training program lasting one to three years for people who are serious about entrepreneurship and gaining the skills necessary to enter the B and I quadrants. In the first year you will learn how to build a business in the S quadrant. In year two or whenever you are ready, you will learn to expand your business in the B quadrant. And in year three or whenever you are ready, you will learn about the I quadrant. Obviously, Rich Dad's GEO program will not be for everyone. It will be challenging and will require an investment of time and money, just as you would expect from any advanced training program. GEO will provide you the teachers, the tools, the training, and the tasks. What you do with them is up to you. If you have an MBA, then you understand that your diploma does not automatically buy you a seat at the board table. You must earn it, just like you must earn the Midas Touch. There are no shortcuts and no guarantees of success.

A Final Thought

Everything of value in life must be earned. It was tough for Robert to get into Navy flight school. Statistics show that the Navy accepts only one out of 3,000 applicants. In the two years it takes to graduate from the program, many of those get washed out before receiving their Navy or Marine Corps wings because they don't have the right focus.

Robert's story of his transition from pilot to combat pilot took even greater focus. The day he climbed into his aircraft, now equipped with guns and rockets, was the day he realized he had to change. Here's a little more of his story:

> After I adjusted to flying a gunship on live-fire missions, my instructor increased the pressure. On the second-to-the-last training flight, he snuck a child's plastic baseball bat into the cockpit. As I rolled the aircraft on the targets in the desert, the instructor began hitting me with his plastic bat on my helmet, on my arms and legs, and across my face. Turning to him, I shouted, "What the hell are you doing?"
>
> "You're dead," sneered my instructor. "You killed us all."
>
> "What the hell are you talking about?" I said, pulling the aircraft out of its dive without firing a shot.
>
> "You lost your focus," said my instructor. "Anyone can fire machine guns and rockets on targets in the desert. In a month, when you are in Vietnam, your targets will be firing back. This plastic bat simulates what it feels like to have bullets ripping through the aircraft. The moment I hit your helmet and face shield with the bat, you lost your focus. You killed us all."
>
> Lesson learned. On my final flight with the same instructor, no matter how hard he hit me with his plastic bat, I held my focus all the way to the target, destroying the target with four rockets and machine-gun fire before pulling out of the dive.

The game had changed, just as changing quadrants changes the game for entrepreneurs. It's not easy. It's uncomfortable. Each quadrant requires different skills and teams, more experience, and greater focus. When you leave the safety and security of the E quadrant, keep your focus, no matter what is thrown at you. If you can survive, keep your focus, and eventually thrive in worlds of the B and I quadrants, you will enter worlds of wealth, success, and power that very few entrepreneurs ever achieve. It takes time, it is not easy, and not everyone makes it, but if you are truly an entrepreneur, what else would you want to do with your life?

Points to Remember | Things to Do

- Specialization is not your friend. You may already be over-specialized. If that's the case, work on experiencing more diverse aspects of business and life. You don't have to know everything about them. Just be exposed to them. Overcome your natural tendency to stay in your comfort zone. Don't stay buried in the details.

- The longer you stay in school, the more specialized you often become. You know more and more about less and less. Break out by taking on different projects, volunteering, doing whatever you can to broaden your horizons.

- Entrepreneurship favors generalists. The more you read, see, hear, and do, the greater your life experiences become. Live your life believing that knowing a little about a lot is a good thing.

- Hire specialists to do the tasks and the work. It's your job to lead them. Use the B-I Triangle as your framework for organizing your company and your leadership. You need to become a master delegator of all tasks on the inside of the triangle so you can do your job of leading the mission and the team.

- Set your sights, and aim high. You never know what you can achieve until you focus on achieving it. Ask yourself honestly, if you had no barriers, how big would you want to be? Now that you know, why sell yourself short? Everything is possible in our highly connected world, once you give yourself permission and focus.

- Get experience before starting your own company. Work to learn, not to earn, and study the companies that are implementing the B-I Triangle the best. Analyze why things go right and why things go wrong.

- Become multilingual. Know the languages of business by diving into them head first. Full immersion will get you fluent faster and make you a better leader who can advise and guide others at all levels of the company.

CHAPTER THREE

THE MIDDLE FINGER
BRAND

*"A brand for a company is like a reputation for a person.
You earn reputation by trying to do hard things well."*

– Jeff Bezos

Are You a Rolex—or a Fake Rolex?
Robert Kiyosaki

"When did you get the Rolex?" asked rich dad.

"I got it last week in Hong Kong," I replied proudly.

"Is it a real Rolex?"

"Well, yeah," I replied hesitantly. "It's real."

With a smirk, rich dad grabbed my wrist and pulled the watch up to his face to take a closer look. "And how much was it?"

"Uh, uh, I got a good deal."

"How much was it?" rich dad asked again.

"Five bucks," I blurted out. "It's a fake Rolex."

"I thought so," said rich dad quietly. There was a long moment of silence. I could tell rich dad was collecting his thoughts.

"Why did you buy a fake Rolex?" rich dad finally asked. "Why didn't you buy a real one?"

"Because real ones are expensive," I answered.

"Do you know why pirates make cheap copies of an expensive watch?"

"Because of price? Because people want a bargain?" I offered up.

Shaking his head, rich dad asked, "Do you know how much the Rolex brand is worth?"

"No," I said, again shaking my head.

"Do you know what the Rolex brand stands for?"

"It means success," I replied. "It means you've made it. It means you've reached the top. At least that's what it means to me. That's why I bought a fake Rolex. I just wanted to look more successful."

"And what does a fake Rolex say about you?" asked rich dad, looking me directly in the eyes.

"It means I want to be successful," I replied. "It means someday I'll own a real Rolex."

"Try again," smirked rich dad. "It means you're a fake. Only a fake would wear a fake. That's what a fake Rolex stands for."

"But a real Rolex costs a lot of money," I protested. "I just wanted to wear a Rolex and I didn't want to spend that much money on a watch. So I bought a five-dollar Rolex. Who will know the difference?"

"You will," replied rich dad. "You know the difference. Deep down you know what the Rolex brand is worth. You know what the brand means. That's why you are willing to be a fake and wear a fake."

"I don't agree," I said. "Nobody can tell the difference. I know. I inspected the watch before I bought it. It looks real."

"But you know it's not real," said rich dad sternly. "You may think you're fooling most people, but you're not fooling yourself. It's what you're saying about you that is important. And right now what you're saying about yourself is 'I'm poor. I'm not successful and I can't afford a real Rolex. So I'll buy a fake because I am a fake.'"

"Why are you being so hard on me?" I asked. "It's just a cheap watch."

"It's more than a cheap watch," said rich dad impatiently. "It's a fake watch, a knock-off, stolen property. If you are willing to buy stolen property, what does that say about you?"

I still did not get why rich dad was making such a big deal out of a watch. I knew it was a fake. I knew it was a copy made by pirates. So what? What's the problem? Who am I hurting?

Continuing on, rich dad said, "If you are going to be a successful entrepreneur, you'd better know and respect a brand. If you are lucky, maybe someday you'll have a brand yourself. Maybe someday your business will become a General Electric, or Coca-Cola, or McDonald's. But if you are a fraud, your business will be a fraud. It certainly won't be a brand."

I did not agree with rich dad and I didn't like what he was saying, but I was old enough and wise enough to know to keep my mouth shut and let the message sink in. I didn't need any more of his wrath. But he wasn't done with my lesson.

"If you are not a brand, you're just a commodity. You're just a faceless product floating in a world of no-name brands."

'What is wrong with being a commodity?" I asked.

"Nothing, if you're happy being a commodity," rich dad replied. "It's the difference between Bobby's Burgers or McDonald's. The McDonald's brand is worth billions. Bobby's Burgers as a brand is worth nothing. Why spend your life building a business and fail to build a brand?"

Catching his breath, or maybe reloading, rich dad let his lesson on brand versus commodity rest for a moment. I understood he wanted me to respect brands and what they stood for. I understood he wanted me to one day be an entrepreneur who turned his business into a brand. He did not want me to become just an ordinary entrepreneur.

"Do you know that just the name 'Coca-Cola' is worth more than the company's entire business? The name is worth more than all the equipment, real estate, and business systems combined," said rich dad, doing his best to have his lesson on brands sink in. "No matter where you go in the world, Coca-Cola is a brand."

"So if I wear a fake Rolex I am stealing from Rolex. Is that what you're trying to say?"

Rich dad nodded his head, adding, "And buying from people who steal from Rolex says, 'I buy stolen goods. I stole someone's good name.' And who wants to do business with someone who is dishonest, cheap, sneaky, crooked, and a phony?"

"Only people who are also dishonest, cheap, sneaky, crooked, and phony," I reluctantly answered.

"If you found out your neighbor with the nice cars and the boat was really a criminal, what would you think of him?"

"Not much," I replied. "I would avoid him."

"That same kind of judgment goes on in business every day," said rich dad. "Honest people do not do business with dishonest people. Your reputation is the foundation of your brand. Guard your reputation with your life. In business, your reputation is more important than your business." With that, rich dad extended his hand towards me, palm up.

I took off the watch and dropped it into the palm of his outstretched hand. Rich dad put the watch on the floor, placed his shoe on top of the watch, and crushed it. Because it only cost five dollars, it crushed pretty easily. I got it.

That was many years ago. Today, counterfeit products, knock-offs, and pirated copies of brands are everywhere. It is a mega-billion-dollar business. There are even counterfeit pharmaceuticals, some of which are actually harmful! Can you imagine how it must feel to lose a loved one because he or she was taking a fake prescription drug, thinking it was the real thing?

In every major city throughout the world, there is at least one street where counterfeit brands and pirated products are readily available. On these streets, you can buy fake Louis Vuitton handbags, fake Nike basketball shoes, fake Armani jeans, and fake Prada sunglasses.

Pirates are entrepreneurs too. They are simply entrepreneurs who steal someone else's brand rather than create their own brand. As long as there are customers who will buy fakes, there will be pirates. If customers were honest, there would not be a business for pirated products. Only crooks sell stolen goods, and only crooks buy stolen brands. Honest people don't do that.

As I picked up the pieces of my crushed fake Rolex, rich dad continued with his lesson, saying, "Very few entrepreneurs ever turn their business into a brand." A brand is priceless. A brand is a promise from the entrepreneur to their customers. A true brand starts in the soul of the entrepreneur and connects with the soul of the customer. It is a relationship, much more than a transaction. In some instances, it is a love affair, a love affair that can go on for years.

"If the soul of the entrepreneur is dishonest or greedy, caring only about the customer's money and not caring for the customer, the entrepreneur's business will never evolve into a relationship. It will remain a transaction. And a transaction is a commodity."

Once the pieces of my fake watch were in the trash can, rich dad said, "The reason so few businesses become brands is because most businesses are primarily in the business of making money. They say they want to do their best for the customer, but for most businesses, that is only hot air. They don't mean it. The more you care about your customer, the better chance you have of your business becoming a brand. Even if your brand does not grow into a Coca-Cola or McDonald's, if you care about your customer, your customer will carry your brand in their heart."

Creating My Own Brand

When rich dad crushed my fake Rolex, my business education into the power of a brand began. I became curious. I did not want to just start a business. I wanted to create my own brand. To do that, I knew I had to study other brands and, at the same time, begin searching for what I stood for, what my customer wanted, and what I wanted for my customers. To do this, I knew I had to begin finding out about myself, and about my business. I had to focus more on giving than receiving. I had to find in my soul, in my heart what I wanted to give to my customers. Once I discovered what I wanted to give, I knew I would find the soul of my business and maybe my brand.

My first big business was my nylon-and-Velcro surfer-wallet business. The name on my products was "Rippers." At first, I thought Rippers was a great name. I was sure it was going to turn into a brand. I thought the name Rippers was cool, unique, distinctive, and spoke to young surfers, the kind of people I knew and loved. Surfers were people like me, so I could relate.

Rippers never evolved into a brand. It was the name of my business, a product line, and a trademark but it never evolved into a brand. And maybe that's the point. We didn't do anything to make it a brand.

That's not to say we didn't market it. My partners and I traveled to surfing trade shows, sporting goods shows, and young-apparel shows, selling our new and unique Ripper products. We were doing our best to get our products into stores all over the world. The problem was that we were burning through money faster than money was coming in. It was a tough time. It was a test of our character. All we could handle was managing the business. Who had time to manage the brand?

I was so screwed up and was being buried alive by my own incompetence. Rippers never had a chance to develop into a brand. It had the makings of a great brand name, but a great name without a great company behind the brand is nothing.

Today, there are nylon-and-Velcro surfer wallets for sale all over the world. The product we created was a success, but it failed to grow into a brand. So today, it remains a commodity, a global product line without a brand leader.

Saved by the Brand

The good news is that even though I could not build a brand out of Rippers, I knew great brands when I saw them. Working to save Rippers, I accidentally stumbled into the rock-and-roll industry, a place loaded with amazing brands.

In 1981, the rock band Pink Floyd contacted my Rippers company to see if we were interested in becoming a licensee of the Pink Floyd band (or I should say, brand). Desperate for any business opportunity, I listened to what the band's agent was telling me. He did not know it, but he was saving my business by selling me a brand, the brand of a world-famous rock-and-roll band.

Not familiar with the rock-and-roll industry, I flew from Hawaii to San Francisco to meet with Pink Floyd's licensing agents. The meeting turned out to be a gift from heaven. At this meeting, my education into the rock-and-roll business began. I realized that, not only can a brand be worth a lot to the owners of that brand, but licensees of that brand can make a lot of money too.

Once I saw the light, I was offered similar deals by hot groups and artists such as The Police, Duran Duran, Boy George, Ted Nugent, Judas Priest, and others. Older mega-groups such as The Grateful Dead and the Rolling Stones were also on the negotiating table. Sadly, The Beatles were not available as a licensable brand at the time.

As rich dad made clear to me, you are either a brand, or you are a commodity. To be a brand, you must have a relationship with your customer, and these bands and artists had great relationships with their customers. The licensing agents were offering us a chance to become a part of that relationship between the fans and the recording artists they loved.

The first meeting with Pink Floyd's people and others that followed saved Rippers by giving us access to a market of rock-and-rollers all over the world. It was like opening a door into a whole new world of business, a world I did not know even existed. We were saved because Rippers became associated with some of the most powerful brand names in rock and roll.

We're with the Band

By 1982, the name Rippers had disappeared from my conversation. Rather than say, "Hello, I'm Robert Kiyosaki from Rippers," I would simply say, "I represent The Police and their licensed products." Nobody knew who Robert Kiyosaki or Rippers was, but they did know The Police, the mega rock band. In fact, one of my first dates with Kim in 1984 was to a Police concert. It was neat saying to her, "I have backstage VIP passes to the Police concert. Would you like to go?" In other words, the power of a brand even worked in getting a date with a beautiful woman who would one day become my wife. Sure, she probably just wanted to meet Sting, but being the one who arranged it, some of that cool was bound to rub off on me.

The Power of the Real Brands

Rippers started out in the surfing and sporting goods industry. The problem was that the surfing and sporting goods business was soon crowded with products similar to my Ripper products, all commodities, not one brand leader. When you're a commodity, then price matters. Since my competition was just like me, a commodity, then retailers beat all of us up on price. Why should they pay more for my product when they can get the same thing from the next guy for a buck less?

When we entered the rock-and-roll business and began capitalizing on brands, people paid the price we asked. All the stores asked was, "How soon can you get us some product?" Pink Floyd didn't license their products to just anyone. A product carrying the Pink Floyd brand was worth more than one that didn't.

Becoming a licensee of mega rock bands gave us exclusivity in a massive worldwide market. Our only competition was the brand pirates, the little criminals who stood just outside the concert entrances, selling their pirated, non-licensed products to rock fans as they left the concert. These little pirates were no different than the person who sold me my fake Rolex. Nervously, they would sell their pirated products, looking over their shoulders, hoping to make a few bucks before the guards at the concert ran them off the property. Just like criminals, they were always waiting to be busted.

At the same time, my company was selling legally licensed rock-and-roll products inside the concert halls. We were also in music stores and department stores all around the world. We were in legitimate businesses because we were legitimate. We were not pirates. My five-dollar Rolex was coming back to me and proving to be a very important lesson about the importance of being legitimate, playing by the rules, and harnessing the power of real brands.

It Wasn't Just about the Money

Working with the rock bands gave me insights into the relationship between a band, their music, and their customers.

It was a relationship, not just a money transaction. Because the bands had a relationship with their customers, selling licensed products was easy. In fact, we didn't have to do much selling at all when people did a lot of buying. At concerts, fans would line up to buy anything with the band's name printed on it. "Line up" is actually not accurate. Picture a shark feeding frenzy. Fans would crowd our tables, wave their credit cards, hand us lots of cash, and say, "I'll take one of those, two of that, and do you have any of those left? I'll take it." They wanted to take home with them a piece of Pink Floyd, Duran Duran, The Police and the other artists they loved. They wanted to make those brands and those bands more a part of their lives.

Different bands had different customers, and the bands had to be true to their own unique customers. For example, the fans of Duran Duran were different than the fans of Judas Priest, Van Halen, or Boy George. They wore different clothes and they used a different language. They just acted differently, and probably were very different attitudinally. If a band stopped being true to themselves, their music, and their customers, business dropped off, sales became difficult, and profits declined. If they put out an album that messed with the fans, we noticed it. When a band came back on track with the next release, bringing out hit songs their fans wanted, business picked back up. Talk about the market giving you feedback!

One of my personal favorite bands of that time was the girl band, The Go-Go's. I loved their music, their sexiness, and their fans. The problem was that their fans did not buy my products. My products were targeted to boys and young men. Very few of my customers were man enough to wear The Go-Go's products. I passed on that band, even though I loved the brand and their music.

The End of Rock and Roll

By 1984, my love affair with rock and roll was ending. While I still loved the music, I was tiring of the business. Something inside of me was changing. I was growing restless, often irritable, and less patient. I had learned my first lesson on the power of brands, and it was time to move on.

While visiting my factories in Korea and Taiwan, something inside of me snapped. I saw everything clearly, and I could not do it anymore. In my factories, I had young boys and girls working in hot, humid sweatshops producing rock-and-roll products that made me richer and those kids sicker.

In one normal-sized room, the sweatshop operator had built two mezzanine floors. Rather than allow workers eight feet of headroom, the young workers had to squat, working in a space about four feet high. Hunched over, they would silk-screen the bands' logos on pieces of cloth, inhaling the toxic fumes being emitted from the cloth and the inks, all within inches of their faces. The fumes were worse than sniffing glue or spray paint, as some kids would do in the West to try to get high. These kids were in it 8 to 10 hours a day, every day.

In another room, there were rows of young girls sewing my hats and wallets into rock-band products. When the sweatshop operator indicated I could have any one of the girls I wanted for sex, the music died for me. I was out of the manufacturing business.

Watching hundreds of kids destroying their lives for a paycheck, I asked myself, "What good am I doing? What good do my products provide? How do my products make the world a better place to live? What value do my products add?" When my questions went unanswered, I knew I had my answer.

I knew it was time for me to find out what I stood for. It was time for me to find out what I cared about. It was time to find out who I was and what made my life worth living.

In December of 1984, Kim and I left Hawaii with two suitcases and nothing more. We moved to San Diego, California. We were beginning our lives as teachers, teaching people to be entrepreneurs, not employees like the kids in the sweatshop. Kim and I were becoming teachers outside the traditional school system. This meant we had no government support or credibility. Traditional schools would not touch us. We had to depend upon our reputation, doing a good job, and giving our students what they wanted. If we were good, students did our marketing for us. If we were bad, they didn't, and no more money came in.

The worst year of our lives was 1985. That year tested our souls, our dreams, and our plans. It was December of 1985 before Kim and I received any money from our new education company. We survived from December of 1984 to December of 1985 on next to nothing. We took life one day at a time. All I know is we operated on faith. Always in the nick of time, something good would happen, and we would continue on, living on very little.

Looking back, it seems our faith was being tested. God, or whoever is running the show, wanted to know if we were committed to being who we were. In other words, were we trustworthy? Would we be true to our brand, or would we give up when things got tough—when the money ran out?

When you read the stories of entrepreneurs, a great number of them have gone through these periods of trials, tribulations, and a testing of faith. I believe it is through this test of faith that a brand is born.

Bill Gates of Microsoft was tested when the U.S. government challenged him, accusing Microsoft of monopolistic practices. Steve Jobs was tested when he was fired from Apple, the company he founded. He was replaced by a more corporate CEO who nearly destroyed the company. When Steve stepped back in, Apple as a company and a brand took off. Facebook founder, Mark Zuckerberg, faced one of his greater tests when the movie *Social Network* suggested that he stole the idea of Facebook. I do not know if Mark Zuckerberg stole Facebook. I just know that being accused of stealing the business you own cannot be easy, no matter how rich you are.

The $4 Million Test

In 2000, after appearing on Oprah's program, I received a call from a famous company that sells mutual funds, asking me to endorse their products. I politely refused, saying that the Rich Dad brand was not compatible with mutual funds. When I refused, the company's agent tested my faith by saying, "We are prepared to offer you $4 million over four years if you will endorse our mutual fund."

A million dollars a year for four years was tempting, but I turned the offer down. Endorsing a mutual fund would not be true to the brand or to the people who believe in the Rich Dad message.

If I had endorsed the mutual fund company, in my mind, I would have looked like a traitor to my readers, a turn-coat, a man who would do anything for a million dollars a year, even sell out his own company and his own soul. It would be like wearing that fake Rolex again.

Testing Never Ends

The Rich Dad brand has been tested a number of times. The first test came in 1997 when *Rich Dad Poor Dad* was first published, stating, "Your house is not an asset." Many real estate agents stopped sending me post cards after that comment. I received hate mail and was publicly accused of not knowing what I was talking about. Many financial experts called me a "quack." Today, with millions of people losing their homes or owing more than their homes are worth, all too many people sadly now know why their home is not an asset.

I did not state, "Your home is not an asset," to win a popularity contest. I am not a politician who wants your vote. I am not a real estate agent trying to sell you a house. I stated those words because I was being true to the brand, true to who I am. I am in the financial-education business, a person who wants you to know the difference between an asset and a liability. If you buy assets before you buy liabilities, you can live in any house you want.

Another test came after I wrote *Rich Dad's Prophecy*, published in 2002. In that book, I predicted the biggest stock market crash in history was coming. I also stated why I thought the mutual fund industry was going to be the cause of the crash, and why millions of investors would never be able to retire.

Once *Prophecy* came out, publications that profit from mutual fund advertising came after me. *Smart Money*, a financial magazine, sent a young reporter to observe me teaching in a large mega-church in Atlanta. The young female reporter stayed through the whole two-day event. A few months later, she stated in her article that I went to a poor black church in Atlanta and took money from poor black people. She wrote this in her magazine, even though she knew I raised over $385,000 that weekend and left every dollar with the church. I did not take any money for travel expenses or for the cost of products sold. After the *Smart Money* magazine article came out, I was even happier I did not take the $4 million endorsement money offered by the mutual fund company.

As you know, the financial services industry is a powerful force operating behind and profiting from the current financial crisis. They have the power to use taxpayer dollars to bail them out of their mistakes and cover their fraudulent practices. They have arms that reach far and wide. They are not people you want to mess with. Personally speaking, I am glad I do not need to count on mutual funds for my financial survival. Given the choice between buying mutual funds or a fake Rolex, I would take the fake Rolex.

In 2006, Donald and I came out with our first book together, *Why We Want You To Be Rich.* We wrote the book because we are concerned with the collapse of the middle class in America. We stated that bad investments and mismanagement of our government were destroying the lives of many people. We wrote about the coming economic crisis and what people could do to not be victims of the crisis. We wrote about inflation making the lives of millions of people more difficult. And we endorsed the idea of financial education as one way to get out of the crisis.

Again, the financial services industry came after us. This time, it was the *Wall Street Journal.* Their direct quote was: "Make no mistake. This is provocative stuff. But don't rush to dump your [mutual] funds quite yet." That was in response to Donald's and my commentary about how mutual funds will be inadequate to fund the majority of Americans' retirement. They made that statement on October 11, 2006, and they didn't seem to believe there was anything to worry about. A year later the market began its free fall. I still predict it will not be the last time this happens.

On March 18, 2008, I appeared on CNN with Wolf Blitzer. He wanted to know if the financial crisis had passed. Rather than say what he may have wanted me to say, that "things will be fine and the worst is over," I instead predicted that Lehman Brothers was in big trouble. On September 15, 2008, Lehman Brothers declared bankruptcy, the biggest bankruptcy in history.

Be True to Yourself

My point for telling you about my personal challenges with the financial services industry is to encourage you to be true to yourself. For me, it was not easy turning down a $4 million endorsement deal. It was not easy saying, "Your house is not an asset." It was not easy predicting the biggest stock market crash in history. It was not easy saying with Donald that the middle class was being wiped out due to government and financial incompetence. It was not easy predicting on worldwide television that the financial crisis was not over and that Lehman Brothers was collapsing.

If I had not said what I said, and done what I did, then I would not be true to myself or my brand. You can't help but notice that Donald is true to his brand. When you walk into his New York offices on Fifth Avenue, his offices are his brand. He makes no apologies for who he is and what he stands for. Neither should you.

One reason most entrepreneurs fail to evolve their businesses into a brand is because money is more important than their brand. Most entrepreneurs will say anything you want to hear, just so you like them and hopefully buy their products or services.

It takes guts to be a brand. It takes guts to stand for what you believe in, even if it is not popular. You cannot be all things to all people if you want to be a brand.

Join the Marine Corps

In the late 1960s, the U.S. military needed pilots for the Vietnam War. Word went out that the armed services were having a combined recruiting meeting for potential new pilots. Three of my friends and I went to the large meeting on Long Island, New York, to listen to the different branches of the service pitch us on why we should join their branch of the service.

An Air Force pilot went first, telling several hundred young future college graduates why the Air Force had the best training and best aircraft to fly. He also showed us pictures of beautiful Air Force bases with golf courses and swimming pools. I thought I was at a presentation for a new resort development, not pilot training.

The Navy pilot went next, telling us about the excitement of flying off an aircraft carrier. It was high adrenaline.

The Army pilot went on about flying large transport helicopters in Vietnam, aircraft like the Sky Crane. He showed pictures of these giant Sky Cranes lifting tanks out of the battlefield.

The Coast Guard pilot shared his experiences of saving lives at sea with his helicopter. He showed pictures of people being hoisted off their sinking sailboat into the safety of a Coast Guard helicopter.

The Marine Corps pilot was last. He stood up and simply said, "Look here. If you want to save people's lives, join the Coast Guard. If you want to kill people, join the Marine Corps." He stepped down, not showing any pictures.

Three years later, I was flying my Marine Corps helicopter gunship off an aircraft carrier, my first combat mission into Vietnam. The Marine Corps had kept their brand promise, just as they have been doing since 1775.

Rolex and the Marine Corps

So what does a fake Rolex and the Marine Corps have to do with the power of a brand?

The answer is—everything. Once rich dad crushed my fake Rolex and I began studying brands rather than pirating a brand, I realized how much of my life has been affected by brands. I knew why I drove Harley-Davidson motorcycles, Ferraris, Porsches, and Bentleys, and why I preferred Prada over Brooks Brothers. I knew why I chose the Marine Corps over the Coast Guard or Air Force, and why I would never again wear a fake Rolex or a fake Ralph Lauren polo shirt.

A brand speaks to that unique, different, and authentic person inside us all. If I stole a brand, then the pirate in me was my brand.

Today, Rich Dad is an international brand. My company does not own manufacturing factories or classrooms. Rich Dad is a brand, a brand that speaks to a specific group of individuals, individuals who want the same things I want.

Keep Your Promise

Donald Trump is true to himself and his brand. That is why the Trump brand is worth so much. The Trump name on a building increases the value of the building by at least 40 percent to 50 percent.

The Trump brand and the Rich Dad brand can stand side by side because both companies value financial education for a better quality of life, not just for the super rich, but for anyone willing to learn.

Yet a brand is more than a name. A true brand cannot be copied because a true brand is more than a product. It is a promise, a reflection of the entrepreneur's body, mind, and spirit.

Remember, you cannot be all things to all people. You can never make everyone happy, so you may as well make yourself happy— happy to be unique, different, giving to others what you want yourself, and doing what you have been put on this earth to do.

If you keep your promise and give people the same things you want, you may be one of the few entrepreneurs who turns their business into a brand.

What's in a Name?

Donald Trump

When I started out in real estate development, my father's name was known in the boroughs of New York City, but not in Manhattan. He had been building housing developments and had become very successful. As a teenager, he had an interest in construction and took carpentry classes.

At the age of 16, he built his first structure: a two-car frame garage. He then established a business building prefabricated garages for $50 each, and he did well. A year after he graduated from high school, he built his first home. He quickly became successful building modestly priced brick houses. The Trump name became known for reasonable prices and high quality.

My father's reputation was solid. I had him as an example of what quality should be and how to achieve it—by scrupulous attention to detail and integrity on all levels. I worked with him in those early years, and I never forgot those lessons. He worked every day and would take us along on the weekends to review the progress. Because of his training as a carpenter, he could always distinguish great work from mediocre work and would point out those details to us. When he told me, "Know everything you can about what you're doing," he was speaking from experience.

A brand stands for your reputation. My father knew that, and Robert is right on target when he says a true brand is more than a product. It's a promise. The Trump brand stands for the gold standard worldwide, and that's a promise we work to keep intact, just as my father did. Robert's hard work to establish the right product took a while, and he was sincere in his attempts to present the best product he could. He achieved his aim.

With my experience working with my father as my early training in branding, I went on and established the Trump name in Manhattan and then nationally and internationally. Much as Robert had his rich dad to point things out to him, I had my father, Fred C. Trump, as a mentor. He often emphasized how important it is to love what you do.

Success most likely won't happen otherwise. He was also efficient and gave me his four-step formula for success:

1. Get in.
2. Get it done.
3. Get it done right.
4. And get out.

That's exactly how he worked. His comprehensive approach to business has always stayed with me. Working with him in those early years and watching him in action was a great education, unparalleled actually. It proves that having an example is a great way to learn, and it's one reason I try to set the example in my organization. People learn by watching as well as listening.

Today, the Trump brand is firmly established as representing the highest quality available anywhere. When you think Trump, you think quality. That didn't happen by accident. It has been a conscious decision since day one, and we work at it daily. For example, when we're working on a new project, we do our research. In Scotland, we not only hired geomorphologists to study the sand dunes, but also made significant improvements in the plan to protect the local wildlife: the creation of three artificial holts for otters, badger protection, new habitats for birds, the erection of nest boxes and bat boxes, the creation of new slacks, plant and habitat translocation, and seed collection to maintain young dune slack habitats. And that's just a short list of how comprehensive we had to be to deliver the absolute finest quality. With this project, the finest quality meant being environmentally sensitive. Nothing, from the wading birds to the Black-headed Gulls, was a minor issue to us.

It's true. Being the best requires full-time attention and application. Mess it up, and it will be in the papers. The fact that I am of interest to the media keeps my name circulating on a daily basis. They are going to write about something. My job, and the job of those around me, is to keep the message one of quality.

The Apprentice also enhances the Trump brand recognition, even in countries where we do not have development projects. I get a lot of publicity, good and bad, but that comes with the territory of being famous. Being a target is something to deal with. But if I wasn't successful, I wouldn't be a target to begin with. After a while, you develop a thick skin when it comes to criticism, whether it's about your hair or your latest building. Any entrepreneur who becomes very successful will be subject to scrutiny as well as criticism. Your critics will surface very quickly and you'll be judged for everything you do, as well as what you don't do, so be prepared for that. The plus is that your name becomes more familiar and the brand becomes more established, provided you're offering the highest-quality goods.

Through my experiences with the media, I've realized that being true to yourself means you are operating from a very solid base, which will give you a lot of power over any negatives thrown your way. That's worth repeating: Be true to yourself!

When Robert used the example of his fake Rolex, it reminded me of all *The Apprentice*-type shows that tried to make it after our initial success. When something is successful, there will always be copycats. You will want to be prepared for that. In the case of *The Apprentice,* none of the copycat shows succeeded. *The Apprentice* was a formula that worked for us, for the Trump brand, but somehow it didn't translate well with other people at the helm. To me, it seemed the whole format didn't fit with who the public thought those other people were. It didn't fit with their brands, and then, of course, the concept had already been done. The other shows weren't different enough to build their own brands. *The Apprentice*, by contrast, was developed with the Trump brand and The Trump Organization in mind, and we were behind the show in every way. That has made it rock solid. When we do an episode of *The Apprentice*, our team is not only completely organized, but also open to creativity and surprises. That's one great thing about being an unscripted show. The only thing predictable is the professionalism of the teams, ours as well as Mark Burnett's.

In one early season during a boardroom meeting, a conflict between several players came up that required me to ask the already-dismissed team to return to the boardroom. Quite honestly, I can't remember what it was, but it was something we couldn't leave just hanging out there. We had to clear up the issue, which took several hours to sort out. Of course, it was edited for television to just a few minutes, but it was a long process. There was no way we could have moved forward without solving the issue, so we took the time. I would have preferred to go home and have dinner, but there's no way I could have ignored the situation. There we were for hours, sorting through the mess, the crew as well as everyone else, just doing their jobs and remaining tuned in. Everything we do we do with care, with an understanding that the show must be entertaining while remaining true to itself and its purpose. What many critics fail to realize is that there is an educational subtext to our show, which gives it a resonance lacking in many other reality shows. Education is and remains a vital tenet of the show, and we receive many letters from schools who use the show as a business class tool.

Man on a Mission

People often ask me if I had a mission in mind when I began The Trump Organization. I don't know if I would have called it a mission at that point, but I knew I wanted a sound base from which to operate. I knew it would be an important aspect of my success, as it would enable me to work as effectively as possible. In the early days, if I had had a mission statement, it would have been concise: "To be the best—in every way." That includes my buildings, my television shows, my golf courses, everything. It has been my personal goal, my focus, and it requires daily application.

Just as having a firm foundation for your brand is important, and a mission statement helps, having the best people surrounding your brand is just as important. When Robert talks about his partners, I think of my employees as well as my business partners and how they have helped the Trump brand become synonymous with the best.

Over the years, I've discovered that for a brand to build, the people surrounding it have to work exceptionally well together. Longevity doesn't hurt, either. I've had people who have been with me for 30 years. My organization became larger as my brand expanded, and despite my fame for saying, "You're fired," I don't like firing people. I'd rather keep them around, provided they are doing a good job. Work ethic matters, too, because our brand-building is constant, never-ending. I've been fortunate in that I seem to attract people with the same work ethic. They understand that they can never let the brand down.

Here's an example of what I'm talking about. We got a call one day from a lady who lived across from one of my buildings. She said our doormen were driving her crazy because, every time she looked out, they'd be polishing something, which she thought was excessive and unnecessary. My buildings are known for being highly maintained, and our theory was that she was just jealous because she wasn't living in my building. The doormen and the maintenance men fully understood the importance of their jobs. Keeping the building in perfect condition is not only critical to our brand, but it's what our residents and guests expect. We were not about to let them down because of one person who was annoyed.

That's a small, but important, example of what I mean. Our team goes above and beyond to deliver the best of everything. There are a lot of things we don't have to do on our projects, and we would still make money on them. We didn't have to redesign the entire golf course in Los Angeles and make it truly spectacular. We could have just fixed the hole that slid into the ocean and been done with it. We didn't have to take as much care as we did with the environment surrounding the golf-links course in Scotland, but we did. We could have done the minimum, ecologically speaking, but we did the maximum. We do what we do because that's what delivering the best means. That's who we are. That's our brand. And the people who work at The Trump Organization take pride in our standard and the part they play in making it real.

When everyone works with that same energy, loyalty, and focus, it makes for smooth sailing all around. I'm definitely in charge, but I expect people to take individual responsibility. I'm not a baby-sitter type. The company has grown larger, but the core ethic is the same—we have a gold standard to maintain. There's an ad that came out years ago with a photo of me and this headline: "I only work with the best." In our company, people have to do their best, and if they understand that, there are no problems. I do my best, and that's what I expect. That's another reason why I expect the gold standard from everyone associated with my brand.

If you are just building your brand, or thinking about it, understand that the integrity of your brand must speak for itself. That should be made clear from the beginning. For example, if you are holding an authentic Fabergé egg in your hand, or the Hope Diamond, it's not really necessary to give a sales pitch. Doing so might make someone wonder if they were the real thing. Keep quality controls on your sales pitches. Desperation never comes off well.

When I was just starting out, I already had the "only the best" attitude going. I always had it in me, and it's something I lived up to. Reputation is something you can't buy. I knew I wanted to establish my brand in the best way possible right away. The renovation of the old Commodore Hotel into the beautiful Grand Hyatt Hotel put me on the map as someone who did good work. Trump Tower cemented that reputation in 1983 and, if you visit Trump Tower, you will still see a remarkably beautiful building.

Building a brand is like building a skyscraper—the foundation comes first and, the bigger the building, the deeper the foundation needs to be. In fact, it helps me to think in construction terms. Do you have a blueprint for your brand? Is the foundation deep and strong enough to support a big structure? Don't leave anything to happenstance. People like safety. A strong brand gives them that safety. When people buy Gucci, they know they're getting high-quality design and materials. They're not taking a chance. If they stay at a Trump hotel, they know they'll have state-of-the-art accommodations and service. From the employees' perspective, a strong brand means pride and security. From the customers' perspective, it means the same thing: pride in owning a great product, and security that the quality will be there. As Robert said, a brand name without a great company behind it is nothing.

Set the Example

I realize that I set the example. My employees and partners see how hard and how long I work every day. They see my standards. That allows the brand to flourish within our company. We don't have long meetings or pep meetings of any sort, because they're usually not necessary. If someone needs to know something, he or she can come ask me. I have an open-door policy. I'm accessible because I like to know what's going on. People understand that my time is limited, so they learn to be brief and to the point. I work fast and so must they. It's a streamlined system and visitors are surprised at how small my core staff is. Everyone pitches in to get the work done. It's a team held in esteem with individual responsibility. I've found that people work harder when they are held accountable, and their confidence level rises along with that. In that sense, I am a teacher and I like to challenge people to do their best. When you get your brand going, that's a good thing to remember. I say that because people respond, not only to the challenge, but to the confidence that is instilled in them when someone believes in their abilities enough to expand their responsibilities. Never judge someone by their job title. You'd be surprised at the talents people can have. Many of my employees have far surpassed what their job titles have implied.

Another important consideration is that, most likely, you will be representing your brand. I represent my brand at all times, and I enjoy sharing my endeavors. I am very much a spokesperson for The Trump Organization and our projects, which is easy for me because I'm truly excited about what I'm doing, and I know my brand is the best. The challenge is making sure that absolutely everything connected with you and your brand is aligned with what your brand stands for. For us, that's being the best. I'd find it hard to believe that every company, yours included, wouldn't want to stand for some aspect of doing good work, so keep in mind that everyone and everything connected with your brand represents you, and your reputation is at stake at all times. It can be a doorman who makes an extra effort, and then someone who doesn't. People can be very critical, and rightly so in some circumstances. Service is a big part of my brand. My customers pay for the best, and they deserve to get the best at every level. Every mistake, no matter how small, is a reflection of you and your brand. Learn from it so it doesn't happen again. Keeping your level of excellence requires diligence at all times.

Being True to Your Brand and Yourself

I like when Robert says to be true to your brand and to yourself. He's also right when he says you cannot be all things to all people if you want to be a brand. You have to decide what it is you want to be known for. You have to be true to yourself. You have to please yourself first. I know we've all heard that before, but otherwise, what are you doing it for? But be warned. Like I said, not everyone will agree with the stand you take. A lot of people like me, and a lot of people don't. That's okay, because my brand is solid and so am I. I can take the negative commentary because the positive impressions are so superior to the reports of the detractors. But I will set the record straight when it might cause damage to my brand or my reputation. People know I'm a fighter in that sense, and they will think twice before going after me, because I'll go after them with everything I've got. When it comes to building your brand and protecting it, you've got to set boundaries. Robert mentions the periods of trials and tribulations, and I agree. Just realize that those experiences are to be expected, especially as your success escalates, and that each situation should be dealt with individually. Being a brand requires being tactical, as well as being strategic.

Years ago, an article came out about me in *The New Yorker* that was basically a hatchet job. I was very angry and was going to call the editor to complain. Then I realized that would be adding some big numbers to their sales because it would end up being a very big story, instead of just a badly written article that would pass in a few weeks. When reporters called me about the story, I'd say it was so long and boring that I couldn't even finish it. No reaction was the strongest reaction in this case. I eventually wrote a letter to the editor after the magazine was no longer on the stands, and I made it clear I was unhappy with "the long and boring story" and couldn't keep my eyes off the Knicks game on television long enough to finish it. I also advised them never to ask me to do another story with them.

Another article deserved a response and the letter I sent won Best Letter to *The New York Times Book Review*, as judged by *New York* magazine. I ended it with good wishes that the writers of the mediocre article about me might astonish us someday by writing something of consequence. There are boundaries to be considered and sometimes a light-handed "toughness" proves useful.

Robert speaks about his various partners over the years. My projects can be huge and involve a lot of partners, too: contractors, designers, architects, managers, general staff, and so on. As he mentions, it matters very much that the fit be a good one. When I have someone design a golf course, for example, we have to have the same vision. Their technical ability is necessary, of course, but more importantly, we have to click, or a lot of time and money will be wasted. That goes for every level of person you're working with.

At this point in my career, I don't need to make more money. I love what I'm doing and I care about the Trump brand, but I am not money-driven. That's why I have a lot of long-standing relationships. I care about the people I deal with, and I care about my customers as well. As Robert mentions, if you don't care, what you will have are merely transactions, not relationships. It's part of building your reputation, which should be foremost in your mind right from the start when it comes to building your brand.

As most people know, I'm known for being candid, and sometimes even blunt. I don't see the point of being politically correct if that means actually being incorrect. I speak what I think. I'm not always popular because of it, but I can't operate as a fake. That doesn't mean I make a career of being adversarial for no reason. I'm also known as being a great negotiator, which means seeing both sides of the story and working towards a mutually beneficial situation for everyone. So there's a fine line you have to tread as an entrepreneur, which translates to life and any kind of business. Being circumspect is something I strive for.

As an example, I have a fantastic building in the Financial District, 40 Wall Street. It's the tallest building in lower Manhattan and a beauty. I had watched that building for decades before making my move to buy it, and when I did, I paid $1 million for it. I watched and waited until the time was right to make my move, and it's now considered one of the best real estate deals ever made in New York. But it wasn't an overnight success story. I waited a long time. At one point, I asked the owners who purchased it in the early 1990s if they'd be interested in a possible partnership, but they were more interested in making 40 Wall Street the downtown equivalent of Trump Tower— including an atrium. What they would do with the steel columns that held up a 72-story building is something that did not occur to them. The structure of the building required steel columns from the ground up, and building an open atrium would not be possible. I was astonished and, at the same time, hopeful. They obviously didn't know what they were doing.

Sure enough, three years later in 1995, the owners wanted out, which put me in a great position. They accepted my terms without question, and 40 Wall Street was mine. I also flew to Germany to meet with Walter Hinneberg to restructure the ground lease which he held. There were a lot of details, one being whether the building should be a residential property (which everyone advised) or to keep it as a great business address. My gut went for the business address, and it has turned out to be a tremendous success. Plus, it's beautiful, and the tallest building in Lower Manhattan. I knew it would be a fantastic addition to the Trump brand of great buildings, and I was right.

Knowing your brand and keeping it intact as you progress requires diligence and focus. I'm big on focus because, when I had a financial turnaround in the 1990s, the number-one lesson I learned is how important focus is. That was the point of the previous chapter and is what the index finger represents. I had lost my focus, and the results were all too obvious. I was attending fashion shows in Paris, traveling around the world, and socializing, and I wasn't working as hard as I should have been. I got a little lazy. But the ultimate wake-up call was when both the *Wall Street Journal* and *The New York Times* had front-page stories predicting my demise—on the same day! Of course, the story was picked up worldwide in a flash. It's a day I won't forget. But I got my act together, and I'm far more successful now than I was then because my focus is definitely in place—personally, professionally and with my brand. Today, I don't allow for distractions and, because of that, I can manage a lot of businesses at once. The Trump brand remained intact during the rough times and from that we moved forward and expanded with new vigor.

Is Bigger Better?

Let's talk about brand expansion. I believe your brand can expand, but the integrity must remain the same. I've expanded into the entertainment business, golf-course development, a hotel collection and many other things, but the common denominator is always there: gold-standard quality. Keep your brand standard in mind, and your expansion will seem possible as well as gratifying. It doesn't mean it will be easy. The golf-links course in Scotland at times was intensely difficult. Just the fact that we were operating in a foreign country was enough, but there were many different factors involved. This brings us back to being true to yourself, which equals being true to your brand. That's the solid foundation that stands the test of time and tribulation that will keep your brand flourishing.

Working Your Brand

I've always been the spokesperson for my own brand. When your brand begins to build, you too will be faced with opportunities for greater recognition. Being in the public eye as a developer in Manhattan started at a relatively young age for me. My projects were big and sometimes surprising to people, and that generated media interest. I became accustomed to the attention, both the positive and sometimes negative. But either way, it helped to establish the Trump brand. It helped people know who I was, and they began to recognize the Trump name. Eventually, I became well known outside of New York as well.

When my first book, *The Art of the Deal*, came out in 1987, it became a bestseller and my recognition factor took an even bigger leap. It was around that time that Mark Burnett read the book. Later, he said it was the catalyst for him to strive to become a success. I know Robert was also impacted by reading it. At that time, Mark was working as a nanny and selling T-shirts on Venice Beach in California. Many years later, he approached me at Wollman Skating Rink, where he was shooting an episode of *Survivor*. He had rented the rink from me for the shoot, and he discussed the possibility of doing a reality show based on me. He asked if he could have a meeting with me in my office, and I agreed. Mark came up and explained his concept of *The Apprentice*, which intrigued me. However, I run a business and was concerned about the time it would take. Mark said, "Donald, I promise you, no more than three hours a week." Believe it or not, I actually believed him! For a prime time show? Anyway, I not only liked Mark but I liked his concept and we shook hands on it. My advisors told me it was a risky thing to do and could damage my reputation, image, and brand. But I'd already agreed, and I had a good feeling about it. I didn't know that 95 percent of all new television shows fail—which is good, or I might not have agreed so readily.

Fortunately, the show was the number-one hit of the season, and my celebrity factor zoomed. I became famous internationally, which had a very positive impact on my business. It also gave The Trump Organization recognition as a company that gets things done and gets them done right. That was, and has remained, a wonderful opportunity for any brand. We're now going into our twelfth season.

I have always been approached to speak at various events and meetings, but after the success of *The Apprentice*, I was asked to do many television commercials and to host *Saturday Night Live*. The invitations to speak approached dozens per week. I was also approached by publishers to write more books. It was a tremendous opportunity for my business to expand and flourish as never before. My point is that I took a very active part in all of these opportunities—because I knew what it meant to the brand. Having a terrific product is not much use if no one knows about it or has heard of it. The name has to get out there, and the recognition should be instantaneous.

When you are presented with similar opportunities to bring your brand to greater recognition, be sure to assess them and take advantage of the chance to broadcast your brand. Never permit yourself to stay in your comfort zone. You should welcome risks. If you're not sure of your brand, then you should get it straight before you do much talking. You should be so sure that your brand is the best, that announcing it worldwide should be exciting, not daunting.

Are You a Communicator?

I'm naturally outgoing. I like to communicate, whether it's with two people in my office or with thousands. I like to tell stories to illustrate my points. If you have a harder time with that, one way to overcome it is to turn your focus onto your audience. What would they like to know? What would make it interesting and fun for them? In a way, it's like negotiating. Try to figure out where they are coming from. Then the focus is less on yourself and your nerves will disappear, or at least calm down.

Being able to speak in public is critical to developing your brand. Otherwise, you should find a spokesperson to take your place until your skills have been honed. The stories I use are usually personal stories. For example, I like to tell the story of a friend who was in the wrong business. Through that story, I emphasize the importance of loving what you do in order to be successful, and this guy was a great example. He worked on Wall Street because his family did, and he thought he should follow suit. The problem was that he was terrible at it, and he looked sick and unhappy. I'm known for being direct, and I finally told him he looked like a loser. Tough words, but I cared about him. I asked him what he liked doing, and he mentioned that he liked taking care of the greens at his golf club. I mentioned golf as a business option. Eventually, he went into it, became successful, and ultimately very healthy and happy.

Once I was several hours late flying in for a speech due to unforeseen events. Once we landed, I had to have a police escort get us through the heavy traffic and the rain. We made it an adventure for the very patient audience of several thousand people by keeping them informed of the seemingly never-ending delays. I was traveling with a crew from *The Apprentice* that was filming the trip and event, so the audience felt part of a reality show that was obviously and certainly unscripted. When I finally arrived, they announced that "Donald Trump has entered the building," and there was a sense of celebration, not dismay, at the long delay. Everyone had a great time. My brand, my name, allowed me even to be excused for being late! It turned a very negative situation for both me and the people who invited me into a positive. That's powerful.

I think representing your own brand yourself is the best way to go. No one knows your product or brand as well as you do. If you can't sell it, who will? You should be capable of representing your own brand in your daily life, as well as in presentations. That's a clue to an airtight brand right there. Entrepreneurs who want to succeed need to know how to be persuasive. The enthusiasm has to be there and it has to be genuine. If you're not comfortable presenting the brand yourself, then find someone who personifies how you want your brand to be perceived.

Image is important and speaks more than the words or fine print that goes along with the product. Think of word association when you say a brand, and the word association will actually become an image if you've executed the branding process well. Aim for instant recognition. The name should be able to say it all if the brand has been thoughtfully and correctly established. For example, say "Chanel" and the image will precede any words, as will "Gucci." And "Trump."

This is when your brand starts working for you. Ultimately, to say a name and have it work as an instant advertisement or visual is your brand at work. You may be just setting the foundation, or maybe it is already set. Once it's up and running, you'll see. It will save you a lot of time. Introductions and explanations won't be necessary. With a brand, you won't have to hunt down opportunities either. They will come to you. What's in a name? A lot! And that's the Midas Touch.

Distilling It Down: Brand

Many entrepreneurs work hard building a business, but only a few build a brand. Building your business into a brand is essential to developing your Midas Touch. Whether you realize it or not, your brand can be many times more valuable than your business. For example, the Coca-Cola brand is worth much more than all the bottling plants, equipment, and capital goods making up the business. Coca-Cola used to be the most valuable brand, but today it is Google. Will Facebook surpass Google in the future? Who knows?

If your business is not a brand, it is a commodity. There are many hamburger businesses, but there is only one McDonald's. There are lots of coffee shops, but there is only one Starbucks. And regardless of whether you love these brands or not, you can't argue with their success. A brand is power. It precedes you and works on your behalf. That's leverage, and in business, leverage is a big advantage. A business that isn't a brand is just "busy-ness." It's a job for you, and a job for your employees. It keeps you busy, but at the end of the day, week, month or year, all you have to show for your efforts is work and, if you played your cards right, profits. Nothing wrong with that, but Midas Touch entrepreneurs want more.

And that leads to a truth in branding: Inside every great brand is the DNA of the entrepreneur who started it all. That DNA is a precious and valuable asset that few companies even recognize they have, until it is lost. If the DNA is not protected, the brand soon dies. This is why so many brands die when the entrepreneur sells their business to a big corporation. AOL and Myspace are recent examples of the death of the entrepreneur's DNA.

What Do You Stand For?

Many entrepreneurs become entrepreneurs simply to make money. A few entrepreneurs are entrepreneurs to make a difference. Which type of entrepreneur are you? You may want to ask yourself this question now, because it matters more than you think in your quest for success.

Kathy Heasley, a brand-development entrepreneur, worked with Robert in writing his sections in this book. Kathy's business, Heasley & Partners, works with new and established entrepreneurs and entrepreneurial companies and shows them how to grow their businesses into brands. Through more than 20 years of guiding entrepreneurs, she has created what she calls Heart & Mind® Branding, her company's own proprietary method of building a brand. Through this process, companies learn how to infuse heart—the higher purpose, the spirit, the soul of the company—into everything it communicates and does. This branding extends beyond marketing and communications and infuses the entire company.

One of her numerous success stories is working with Doug Ducey, an entrepreneur and the driving force behind the success of Cold Stone Creamery, which today is an international ice cream brand.

In 1999 when Kathy first took on Cold Stone Creamery as a client, Cold Stone was a startup ice cream franchise with about 12 employees, 35 stores, and a few million dollars in gross revenue. By the time Cold Stone was acquired less than ten years later, the business had grown to more than 1,400 stores and more than half a billion dollars in gross revenue.

Kathy has these thoughts about entrepreneurs, business, and branding: "People often think a brand is a logo. They think it's an advertising campaign or sales promotion. It is none of those things. A brand is two words: the 'Promise' you telegraph, and the 'Experience' you deliver. A brand is founded on what the entrepreneur stands for. When people see your brand, hear your name, or use your products, those symbols and experiences should trigger in them what you stand for. I'll take it one step further. You, your name, your products, and your service should trigger both an emotional response and an intellectual response in your customer. Heart & Mind Branding is founded on the fact that we all buy with our hearts and justify with our minds. In other words, a brand must be emotional first, logical second."

Questions to Ask Yourself

Successful entrepreneurial businesses have that special something, that magic that will ignite a brand. For Cold Stone Creamery, it was a passion for making people happy, a drive to be the best and deliver the ultimate ice cream experience.

Leaders need to have a fire in their heart, and a good reason for being—the story behind the story—and they must connect with that story and allow it to shine through.

The following are three big-picture, fundamental questions all entrepreneurs should ask themselves:

Big-picture question #1: Why do you do what you do?

Do you know your "why" behind your "what"? You have to have a good reason for doing what you're doing, because people connect with the why. You have to bring that genuineness to life in the brand. Entrepreneurs have to have heart for what they do, because the first mark of a great brand is its genuineness. It's not all about the money. You might be successful as an S, but your "why" won't be enough to carry the business through to a B-quadrant brand.

When people meet us, they can tell there is a very big "why" behind what we each do. After all, both of us are seasoned entrepreneurs and business people. We are both highly successful. Neither of us has to work, but we do. Even though we are both in the money business and enjoy the game of making money, we are not doing it for the money. Money is not our "why." The fact is that if you look deep, both of us are really teachers. We genuinely enjoy teaching people to become the best they can be and live the best life they can. That underlying "why" is behind every book we write, every project we do, every investment we make. We wrote our first book, *Why We Want You To Be Rich,* for no other reason than to enlighten people to how the world works and the threat we are all facing today. We wrote about the erosion of the middle class, why it is happening, and what you can do to make sure you rise to riches instead of fall to poverty. That's teaching, and that's where our hearts are. We want people to live better lives.

Many people have certainly heard of Donald Trump, and the same thing goes for the book, *Rich Dad Poor Dad*. Explore the worlds of business and entrepreneurship and, before long, you'll know exactly who we are. You immediately sense we have a spirit and stand for something much greater than just making money. We live by that old saying, "What you think of me is none of my business." In other words, we do not need your approval to exist. Socially, we are both respectful, often polite, yet you know there is a fire burning in our hearts. We are intense, tough, and mission-driven.

People know who we are behind our images and how that connects with our companies. They see our level of focus, our emotional strength, and our dedication to working hard. Branding is a marathon as much as it is a momentum business. Leaders can't dip in and dip out at will.

Ask yourself these questions:
- What do you want to achieve with your business?
- What gets you up in the morning?
- Have you ever failed?
- Where do you see yourself in five years?
- What do you want your legacy to be?

Ask Yourself

As you ask yourself these questions, call up a friend you trust and have a conversation. Exchange feedback and write it all down. Go through this process more than once. The questions are important. Repeat the process until you become clearer about who you are, why you do what you do, and if you have the fire it takes to become a real brand. Through that process, you'll discover most genuinely what you stand for.

You'll also want to ask similar questions of your customers and employees. When it comes to uncovering the genuine entrepreneur, the genuine company, everyone has a voice.

Big-picture question #2: What problem do you want to solve?

A true business only exists to solve a problem and to make life better. If what you do doesn't benefit others, it's not meaningful. Great brands are not only genuine, they are meaningful, too.

Our brands work well together because they work on the same problems. Although we are very different and come from different ends of the United States, New York and Hawaii, both of us had rich dads. One of us is from a rich family and the other is from a middle-class family, and yet we are both joined at the heart as educators. We are teachers, often sharing a stage together speaking to large audiences, encouraging attendees to go for their dreams. We both have educational television programs: Donald's hit TV show *The Apprentice*, and Robert's TV programs on PBS. We both have financial-education games, lead financial-education companies, and write books. We are doing our best to fill an educational void caused by the lack of financial education in our schools. We know a major problem in society is the lack of financial education. When combined with other forces, this lack of financial education is causing a growing gap between rich and poor along with a shrinking middle class. Job loss, low pay, higher taxes, declining home values, rising inflation, unaffordable medical care, and a lack of retirement savings are all decimating the majority of Americans. We want to be part of the solution. This is why we teach and share our knowledge, so more people can enjoy a better life.

Our principles have been tested. Neither of us will share the stage with other financial experts who say, "Live below your means." We want people to have the financial knowledge to possibly even live above their wildest dreams. Both Mark Burnett, the producer of *The Apprentice*, and Robert were inspired to live above their dreams after reading Donald's book, *The Art of the Deal*. As Donald stated previously, "Mark was working as a nanny and selling T-shirts on Venice Beach in California. It was around that time that Mark read my book." Today, Mark Burnett is the leader in the world of reality television and is wealthy beyond his dreams.

Robert's wife Kim says, "In 1987, we were still in trouble financially. In 1986, we had finally paid off nearly a million dollars in losses from Robert's wallet business. We were at zero. We had no debt, but we had no income. As soon as we heard about Donald's book, we ran out, bought it, read it, studied it, and discussed it in depth. That book changed our lives. It changed our lives because Donald allowed us to see his world through his eyes. He didn't give us answers. He simply opened our eyes to a world of possibilities. That's what great teachers do."

The Trump, Kiyosaki, and Burnett brands are all meaningful in today's world. They solve problems, create jobs, and move us forward in sync with what's happening nationally and globally. Both the Kiyosaki and Burnett brands have been associated with the Trump brand. The results are beneficial to all. Individual brands are powerful, but when they come together, they can become exponentially greater.

Understand what makes your business meaningful by thinking through the following questions:

- What is the problem you want to solve?

- Why is it a problem?

- What causes the problem?

- If your business were gone tomorrow, what would the world lose?

- What makes you think you can solve the problem?

- How does your product or service solve the problem?

- How does your product or service make your customer's life better?

- What do you think your customers really need from a company like yours?

Again, take the time to ask yourself these questions. Then ask your friend to ask you these questions. Repeat the process until you are clear on what makes you meaningful. That's the second trait of a great brand.

Big-picture question #3: Who or what is your competition?

Every business has competition and, when building a brand, you must be different. In fact, that's the third characteristic of a great brand—different. Too many businesses are 'me too,' and those will never rise above the fray and break through. When we hear someone say, "My product has no competition because we are so unique," we know we have a dreamer in front of us, not a businessperson. There is always competition,even if the competition is the fact that your customer doesn't know you exist. Ignorance can also be a competitor.

Most people have too narrow a focus. They only see their product or service, the top of the B-I Triangle. Often, they fail to see the full scope of the 8 Integrities of a Business. If they cannot see the entire B-I Triangle, they have blind spots in their vision of the world, and they will never find or be able to fully create their points of difference.

Often by being genuine to who you are and meaningful to the people you serve or wish to serve, you are, by definition, different. So few companies have a grasp of this, which means you stand out. Working in a company with purpose is more fun, more meaningful, and more satisfying.

To uncover a company's point of difference, seek to understand such things as:

- Why should people choose your company over others?

- Can you state how you're different in fewer than 25 words?

- Can your employees state your difference, and are they all saying the same thing?

- What is your presentation style?

- Are you confident in sales situations?

- Are you confident on stage?

- What things do your company, and only your company, "own"?

- Are you "Google-ready"? When people Google your company to check you out, do the results enhance your brand?

- How willing are you to change and adapt?

- How fast can you and your organization change?

Ask yourself these questions, and find your own answers. Then you may want to ask a friend to go over the same questions with you and provide feedback. It's important to repeat the process until you are clear on your answers.

If you are an employee, ask the same questions and answer the questions for the leaders of the company you work for. In other words, are your leaders with it, or are they dinosaurs? If you do not like your leaders' answers, you may want to start looking for a new job because you will probably need to look for a new job in the near future.

In today's world of accelerating technology, there is more and more competition for your customer's attention, time, and money. The world of the web is the new world of "Free." How can you compete when everyone is giving away for free or selling at deeply discounted prices what you are trying to sell? Those of us who were born before 1970 may have business wisdom, but we run the risk of not being very tech-savvy, even if we use email and have a Facebook account. For those people born after 1970, they are often more tech-savvy, but lack the wisdom to use it well. Today, entrepreneurs must be both tech-savvy and wise. The entrepreneur who possesses both these traits has a huge competitive advantage.

The world changed in 1989, the year the Berlin Wall came down and the World Wide Web went up. Those events signaled the end of the Industrial Age and the beginning of the Information Age. Today, your competition is everywhere. Your competition is in everyone's home, office, and cell phone. The cyber world of "Free" is taking down one-time mega-brands such as *TIME* magazine, because *TIME* has no idea how to compete in our new world. On top of that, technology speeds up transaction time. The reason we have 20-year-old billionaires and 50-year-old unemployed, college-educated people is because businesses in the cyber-world can sell to more people faster for lower prices and with fewer employees. They know how to build a name for themselves, their companies, and their products online. It is easier than ever before, but it's also harder than ever before. The Internet gives us access, but because it gives access to everyone, it clutters the playing field. It takes strategy and steady work to break through. But without a brand, you are lost in a massive, bottomless sea.

The Internet can be a dangerous place, and it's easy for consumers to fall prey. Brands bring safety and security to this unbridled world. If your brand can flow easily between cyber and real and back again, all the better. In fact, that adds to its credibility. A brand that can connect, compete, and transact business at high speed in the real world and in the cyber world has great potential.

Great Brands

Great brands are:
• Genuine
• Meaningful
• Different

Practicing what you preach is all about being genuine: living your words, walking your talk, and talking your walk. A fake Rolex makes the point that, if you fake it on the outside, you're probably faking it on the inside. Anyone who thinks people don't pick up on phoniness is kidding themselves. If your customers don't pick up on it right away, they will eventually. As that old saying goes, "You can fool some of the people some of the time, but you can't fool all of the people all of the time."

In today's economy, people are very sensitive to brand promises, price, and value. This means people want to know that you are caring more about them than what you are selling them. Today, you, your business, and your brand must first let people know what you care about and that you care about them. If you don't, your competitor will. You see, a business is not about money. A business is about caring. If you do that—genuinely care, fulfill your brand promise with an outstanding experience, and operate 24/7 from everywhere—money will come pouring in.

Great brands start at the heart of the organization, then permeate through everyone in the organization, and then go out to the public.

All our military branches—the Army, Navy, Air Force, Coast Guard, and Marines—are great brands. Yet the brand message of each military branch is different. Once a person decides to join a certain branch of the military, he or she doesn't simply put on a uniform. No, before that official uniform is donned, the future soldier is taken apart, stripped of former identities, beliefs, thoughts, and habits. Only then is he or she ready to become a member of the Marines, Army, Navy, Coast Guard, or Air Force. The armed services make sure their people are first branded—mentally, physically, and spiritually.

This branding process is especially true for the Navy SEALs (which stands for Sea, Air, and Land), one of the most elite and prestigious fighting units in the world. The 2,500 SEALs are considered some of the world's finest fighters. SEALs go through an extremely arduous two-year training program before becoming a SEAL. The process weeds out 75 to 90 percent of those accepted into the program. In one of their tests of will, a challenge known as "drown proofing," trainees are bound hand and foot, thrown into deep water, and told to get to the surface somehow while holding their breath. Then they swim 50 meters while still tied up. The worst challenge is "Hell Week," a period where trainees are kept awake for 20 hours a day, performing relentless, physically punishing drills, while constantly being invited to quit. At the end of Hell Week, if they have not quit, trainees are hosed with freezing cold water to induce hypothermia. Then they swim two miles through the ocean. When the trainees emerge from the swim, they are handed a mug of steaming hot chocolate by an instructor, but told they can only drink it if they admit failure and drop out of the program. Many SEALs admit that handing back that steaming cup of chocolate is the hardest thing they have ever done.

Military organizations are some of the most sophisticated brand-builders in the world. A true brand starts from the core, the heart, and permeates throughout the hearts and minds of everyone in the organization and then to the outside world. The best brands become part of our DNA.

When SEAL Team Six (ST6) killed Osama Bin Laden, the power of their brand echoed throughout the world. Many people who had not heard of the SEALs were saying, "Who are those guys?" Since the SEALs abide by a code of silence, their deadly silence has made their brand even more powerful. What does that say about businesses that simply bombard us all with meaningless, loud, obnoxious advertising? It means they are not building a brand. They are being a nuisance.

One of the greatest brand-builders of all times was Attila the Hun. His brand preceded him so powerfully that opposing armies often surrendered before fighting him. Although he was the leader of the Huns from 434 to 453 A.D., people still speak of Attila today. That is brand power, and proof that a brand can build a legacy.

Today, entrepreneurs such as Steve Jobs of Apple, Mark Zuckerberg of Facebook, and Sergey Brin of Google are modern Attilas who are building their brands and their legacies. They have built some of the most powerful brands in world history. When Jobs, Zuckerberg, or Brin move, the world shakes and businesses are forced to change or die.

Even criminal organizations have brands. For example, the name Cosa Nostra brings fear into people everywhere. The same is true for the Yakuza of Japan. In the world of drugs, the Cali cartel and Medellin cartel of Colombia were and are known as leaders in the cocaine trade.

Crooks also have brands. The name Bernie Madoff was once golden in the world of the rich and famous. Today, he is infamous for operating the biggest Ponzi scheme in history. Could the name Bernie Madoff become more famous than Charles Ponzi, the person the Ponzi scheme was named after? Time will tell if, in a few years, what were once called Ponzi schemes become known as "Madoff schemes." In many ways, the name Bernie "Madoff" better describes the crime!

It's important to realize the power and value of a brand. You have to be willing to do what it takes, in both time and money, before you begin the process. Many leaders want to grow, they want to create great companies, but not all of them are willing to do what it takes to make that pipedream become a reality. For many CEOs, affording the time is more expensive than the money.

We realize that branding is a way of life, not an event. We know that it is the brand that enables us to fulfill our life's purpose, so it is worth our energy and time. That may be why we are international brands. We value it.

A Final Thought

Brands are everywhere and in everything. There are global brands and local brands. There are brands for the rich and brands for the not-so-rich and everyone in between. There are brands for kids and brands for adults. Every industry has a brand. For example, in the world of gold, there are American Eagles, Canadian Maple Leafs, Australian Kangaroos, and South African Krugerrands. Although they are gold, they sell for different prices.

In religion, there are many brands and sub-brands. In Christianity there are Protestants and Catholics. In Buddhism, there are Tibetan, Chinese, and Japanese Buddhists. The Dalai Lama, a power brand unto himself, is a Tibetan Buddhist. Inside Tibetan Buddhism, there are sub-brands and sub-conflicts. And in a world of terrorism, we are all aware of the battles between Jews, Muslims, and Christians. Why is there such tension and conflict? The answer is partially explained from the context of brands, sub-brands, and the battle for the hearts and minds of religious followers.

In politics, the Republicans would not have much to say if not for the Democrats. If there were no Republicans, we would not need Democrats. People come together in brands, and are also polarized by brands.

In an increasingly competitive world of business, a world of higher quality at lower prices, a world of rapidly evolving technology and ever faster transaction speeds, building a brand may be more important than building a business. In fact, building a business without a brand is becoming harder every day.

Points to Remember | Things to Do

- Unless you build your business into a brand, you'll never have the Midas Touch.

- Your brand must be genuine, not fake. People can spot a fake.

- A brand is not a logo. A brand is the *promise* you put out there and the *experience* you deliver.

- People buy with their hearts and justify their purchases with their minds. So have the courage to find your heart and put it into your brand.

- Figure out what really moves you. You've got to have the fire in order to have the Midas Touch.

- If you are too cheap to invest in your brand or yourself, then the Midas Touch will elude you. By cheap, we're talking about money, time, commitment, and people.

- Do whatever it takes to improve your public-speaking skills. You'll absolutely need them.

CHAPTER FOUR

THE RING FINGER
RELATIONSHIPS

*"In the end, all business operations can be reduced to three words:
people, product, and profits. Unless you've got a good team,
you can't do much with the other two."* – Lee Iacocca

The Perils of Partnerships
Robert Kiyosaki

"You can't do a good deal with a bad partner."

These words could be the most important words in life, not just in business.

These are more than words of wisdom. These are guiding words, words to live one's life by.

Whenever you find a struggling business, a bad marriage, or an investment gone bad, you will find a bad partner.

This does not mean the person is a bad person, although they could be. It just means they are a bad partner, the wrong person for the task at hand.

The world is filled with good people, but they would not make good business partners. In the institution of marriage, the world is also filled with good people who are married to the wrong person. And if you encounter a truly bad person—a person with low legal, ethical, and moral values—no matter how good you might be, the business or marriage will go bad.

The Ring Finger

The ring finger represents relationships essential to the Midas Touch. If you have bad partners, whatever you touch will turn bad. And if you have great partners, everything you touch turns to gold.

Clowns, Not Partners

In the late 1970s, my nylon-and-Velcro surfer-wallet business was taking off. The problem was that success was costing us money. I began this story earlier in the book. Since our company was always out of cash, I had to keep raising money. We would buy a production run of wallets from factories in Korea and Taiwan and then ship the wallets to the stores after they arrived in our warehouse. Sounds pretty good, right? We were selling product as fast as we could manufacture it. The problem was that we needed to order and pay for more wallets before our customers, the stores, paid us. That's why we were always in cash-flow trouble. We estimated that, on average, we would spend a dollar in April and not see any return on that dollar until February, the next year. It was a ten-month cycle. Cash was flowing out, not in. The more successful we got, the more cash that flowed out and the slower it flowed in.

As the demand for Rippers products grew, our demand for cash also grew. Soon, raising $5,000 to $10,000 was not enough. To keep products flowing to the stores and to build the business, we needed to raise at least $100,000. Since rich dad was the only person I knew who had that much in cash, I called and asked for an appointment.

Rich dad listened patiently to my investment pitch for about ten minutes. Once he heard about as much as he could stand, he politely asked my two partners to leave the room. Once the door was closed, the shouting began. It was one of the harshest tongue-lashings I have ever received.

Rather than refer to my two partners as partners, he called them "clowns." To make matters worse, he was certain one of my partners, my CFO, was weak, dishonest, and potentially a crook. He did not even know the guy. He just did not trust him from the moment he met him.

Although he liked me and my other partner, he did not feel we were good enough to be his partners, and certainly not his money's partners.

"Why should I be your partner?" rich dad asked. "You have no experience, you have no success, and I don't trust either one of you. If you partner with a person I don't trust, this makes me not trust you. It shows you do not know what a good partner is. You guys are clowns, not business people."

The lecture was painful and it seemed to go on forever. Needless to say, we left without the money. I did not speak to rich dad for years after that.

We did raise the $100,000, and rich dad was correct. We were bad partners. The money was gone and the person rich dad did not trust, a CPA with the title of CFO, actually did run off with the money.

More Bad Partners

I wish I could say that experience taught me a lesson. It did, but apparently I needed to learn more because I have lived through it more than once. Over the years, I have gone from bad partner to bad partner which, according to rich dad's assessment, makes me a bad partner.

The pattern of bad partners repeated itself time and time again. I would start a business with a person or persons I thought were good partners. The business would take off. Yet once successful with money coming in, the good person would turn into a bad partner.

It happened in my Rippers business, then the rock-and-roll phase of Rippers, then in my education company, and finally with my partner and her husband in The Rich Dad Company.

In two of the businesses, success revealed bad partners who could not handle success. They were not really bad or dishonest people. They had simply never been successful. When success appeared, so did their character flaws. For example, one partner in a small education company simply started spending money like she was rich. Since she had never had money, seeing so much money coming into the business only released her pent-up desire to go shopping. When she started buying personal items using the business credit card, Kim and

I ended our partnership with her. She was a good person who loved to go shopping.

In some cases, bad partners were dishonest partners. Interestingly, my bad partners in both Rippers and Rich Dad were accountants and attorneys by training, professionals I had hired to protect me from people like them.

Again, I know this makes me look like a fool, and a bad partner myself. I wish my sequence of business start-up, business success, and the unveiling of bad partners were different. I wish I were writing instead about good partner experiences so I could be more positive about it. I thought about being more general and not writing about my poor choices in partners, yet I believe the lessons to you, the reader, are far more important than preserving my ego, or the illusion that I know what I am doing. Like many people, I go from screw-up to screw-up and somehow do okay in between.

Truth Be Told

I might not have survived if I did not have a great wife and business partner in Kim. Since 1985, we have gone through some horrifying betrayals from our partners. If not for Kim and great friends, we might not have survived the financial and emotional devastation we have had to endure. The financial cost has been in the tens of millions of dollars, nearly a hundred million, but the emotional damage has been much, much higher. To see people who were once friends and partners suddenly unmasked, people we worked side by side with for years revealing their lowest of base human behavior, is disturbing. It's something never to be forgotten.

In Vietnam, I thought I saw the worst of the human animal, but the animal I saw in Vietnam is not the same animal I see in business. In Vietnam, fear brought out the animal in a few soldiers. In business, greed and fear drive the human animal. The betrayals in business are more sinister because the betrayal is often against friends and co-workers, not enemies.

Betrayals Are Part of Life

There are two basic types of betrayal. One is criminal or intentional betrayal. The other is betrayal due to incompetence or ignorance. If you can learn and grow from life's betrayals, you have a better chance of evolving into an entrepreneur with your own Midas Touch.

The interesting aspect of all betrayal is that the person who is actively betraying you often feels he or she is the one being betrayed. In other words, that person finds a way to justify betraying you.

Your challenge is to become a better person for it. It may mean you don't retaliate even though you want to. It may mean not fueling the flames and amplifying the betrayal process. It's tough, but the challenge is to become bigger than the person who betrayed you. If you have yet to be betrayed, you'll see a side of yourself you may not have seen yet. If you know you have it in you, you've probably been betrayed in your life.

The pain of betrayal can be so great that your first response may be to want to punish the person who betrayed you. Resist that urge to turn primal, even if you feel justified in doing so. You see, that is what the person who is betraying you is doing. He or she has found a way to justify betraying you, regardless of whether or not you deserved it. In effect, he or she is punishing you for your betrayal, even if you did nothing at all.

In my Rippers business, my CPA Stanley took the $100,000 I raised from an investor and paid off his friends who had invested in the business. When I confronted him, reminding him that we agreed the $100,000 was to buy more products rather than pay back investors, he reacted by saying, "But I had to pay off my friends first." In his mind, he did the right thing, even though he betrayed his partners.

When I explained to him that the $100,000 in products would have been worth $1 million or more in sales, more than enough to pay off all our investors, he would not listen. Once he paid off his friends, he resigned and the business soon collapsed. After Stanley left, he called other investors to tell them how incompetent I was. Soon more and more investors began demanding their money back. Did I want to get back at Stanley? Of course, but I didn't.

It took me two years to rebuild the business and begin paying investors back. It turns out doing the right thing, the hard thing, rather than going bankrupt, was a priceless experience in my development as an entrepreneur. Painful as it was, I became better for the experience. Don't expect to arrive at that kind of insight overnight though. If you're like me, you'll want to get even many times over before you learn to appreciate the experience.

Rich dad could sense Stanley was weak and lacked courage. When the pressure from his friends grew too great, he betrayed his partners and the business.

I do not know where Stanley is today, but I know I am a better entrepreneur because of the $100,000 experience. In an odd way, Stanley helped me develop my Midas Touch. I am more aware now of weak people in business and how dangerous they can be.

As a former Marine, retaliation, pain, and retribution are all part of my character. The Marines have very little tolerance for weak people like Stanley. It was a test of my character to not bring justice to Stanley the Marine Corps way. If you saw the movie *A Few Good Men* starring Jack Nicholson and Tom Cruise, you were afforded a glimpse into the Marine-Corps culture and code of honor. Not retaliating against Stanley was a big step for me.

Rising above situations and getting better although betrayed, has been essential for my personal development. I would say it has been the key to my success. While I still have the same intensity for pain and retribution I developed as a Marine, today I focus that intensity on events and actions that are more positive and more beneficial in the long run.

There is a lot of truth to the saying, "An eye for an eye makes us blind." Rather than take another person's eyes, which the Marine in me would do, I choose to follow the saying, "The best revenge is success." Bad partners have been the firewood in my fire for success. Rather than retaliate, I use my anger to become more successful.

Today, I attribute much of my success to my bad partners, because bad partners taught me how to become a good partner. I have a lot more to learn.

Lessons from Relationships

The following are a few hard-won lessons about partners, people, and relationships, learned along a long and bumpy road.

1. **You can't do a good deal with a bad partner.**
   I repeat this because it is worth repeating. Whenever I find a business, a marriage, or a group struggling financially, I begin looking for the bad partner. More often than not, the bad partner is the leader, a person who might be a good person but a bad business partner.

2. **You get offered a lot of good deals when you are a good partner.**
   This is the positive side of the first lesson. Rich dad taught me that I would never be successful if I remained a bad partner by hanging out with bad partners. He inspired me to be a student of human nature and business, work diligently, and take life one day at a time. He assured me that if I became a good partner, good people and good deals would find me.

   So far, rich dad's promise has come true. Between 2007 and 2010, during my trials with my former partner and a crashing economy, more good deals came to Kim and me than at any time previously. We made a lot of money with good people. If we were bad people with bad reputations, I am certain we would never have been invited to invest with one of the more prominent investment groups in America.

3. **From bad deals come good partners.**
   Through every bad deal, I have met a great partner. I met Ken McElroy, Kim's and my partner on a number of larger apartment projects, through a bad deal.

   Ken, his partner Ross McCallister, Kim, and I have gone on to make millions together.

If not for a bad deal put together by a bad person, Kim and I would never have met Ken. Can you see the pattern? This has happened many times in my career as an entrepreneur. So now I know. Whenever a deal is going bad, I begin to look for my new partner.

4. **Good people can make bad partners.**

Many people want to be entrepreneurs, but they should not be invited to be part of a business, especially a start-up.

Since most people are trained to be E's and S's, employees and specialists, most do not have the experience, education, or emotional maturity to be part of an entrepreneurial business team. The lack of experience, education, and emotional maturity can turn a good person into a bad partner.

A friend of mine has a banquet company. He loves his business because he loves to cook. He spends every waking hour thinking about new recipes and ways to make his banquets more memorable. The problem is that he is not interested in business. He has never taken a course in accounting, marketing, finance, or business law. He is not a student of business, and his business and employees suffer for his lack of business education.

Unfortunately, he thinks he is good at business. No one can tell him anything.

When he wanted to become a part of one of my start-ups, we turned him down. He is a good person, but we did not feel he would make a good partner. I have found this phenomenon especially true with medical doctors and accountants. They feel they are good business people because they did well in school and run their own practices. Unfortunately, I have found that doctors or lawyers who are good at business are the exception rather than the rule. Hence, they make poor partners.

5. **Inexperienced good people don't get invited into the best deals.**
   Since most people have never been part of a successful
   entrepreneurial venture, most people are not invited to join
   in the best deals. They may be invited into bad deals, deals no
   one else wants, but the best deals are not offered to them first.

   Once you achieve success as an entrepreneur and have a good
   reputation, everyone wants you to join them. In other words,
   the more successful you are, the more success chases you. If you
   have some money but have no real-world experience and no
   success as an entrepreneur, the SEC (Securities and Exchange
   Commission) laws prohibit you from investing in the best,
   most profitable, and tax-favored investments.

   The SEC recommends, and often requires, good people who are
   inexperienced to stick with savings, stocks, bonds, and mutual
   funds, even though these investments are among the riskiest,
   highest-taxed, and lowest-return investments in the world.

Priceless Relationships

Rich dad often said, "Business is easy. People are difficult."
I would say this is true for me. Over the years I have met some
horrible people, as well as many wonderful people. I have met great
people like Donald Trump, the Dalai Lama, Steve Forbes, and Oprah
Winfrey—people I would never have met had I not started my first
business and continued on, learning from my mistakes after the
business failed.

When you look at the following diagram of the B-I Triangle—
8 Integrities of a Business, it is easy to understand why rich dad said,
"Business is easy. People are difficult."

A true business requires a minimum of eight different skill sets, ideally eight different people all working for a unified goal. While there are many reasons why 9 out of 10 businesses fail in the first five years, the entrepreneur's inability to focus on the 8 integrities and produce a profitable result is what causes most businesses to ultimately fail.

One reason I started my nylon-and-Velcro surfer-wallet business, even though I knew the probability of my failure was high, was because I did not know of a better way to learn to deal with different people, most with some success and strong egos. I suspected that if I would stick to the process, taking the good with the bad, learning and growing rather than retaliating, I might evolve into a good partner. I continue in the process today, simply because I have a lot to learn. Learning to deal with different people seems to be a process without end, and I can always learn more. The good news is that the better I get at relationships and meeting good partners, the easier and happier life becomes and the more my wealth goes up.

Of all the five fingers in the Midas Touch hand, I believe the most important finger is the ring finger because, if you learn to become a good partner, you will meet some of the greatest people, people you might not have met had you not decided to travel the rocky road of business.

Remember, you can't do a good deal with a bad partner. If you become a good partner, the world is filled with great deals and great partners.

A Final Thought

A few years ago, I was shown into Donald's office while he was still on the phone finishing up a call.

"Are they good people?" Donald asked the person on the other end of the phone. "I don't care how good the deal is. I have plenty of good deals. I want to know if they are good people."

After listening to the other person's response, Donald said, "I'm glad to hear that. If they're good people, I'll go forward." With that, he hung up.

Donald looked up at me and said, "At our age, we don't have time to do business with bad people. We don't need the money, and we don't have the time. Besides, business is tough enough. Why should we do business with bad people? It's more fun doing business with good people."

With that, he looked at me and asked, "So what are we working on next? Let's have some fun and make some money."

Strong Relationships Are the Key
Donald Trump

I've had thousands of business relationships over the years. I've found that relationships and reputation are closely intertwined.

Sometimes it takes years to see someone's backbone, or lack of it, and sometimes it is readily apparent. I have always liked Henry Ford's quote: "You can't build a reputation on what you're going to do." And you can't build a reputation if your relationships or partners aren't right. I know Robert would agree with that one. I've had potential partners who were full of great ideas—and short on delivery. And I've had great partners who delivered all the way.

The Best Partner

When I started out, I had a tremendous partner—my father. That's hard to beat. We had a great relationship. I worked on his construction sites during the summer. I have already mentioned his attention to detail, which I have emulated, and I remember his picking up and recycling unused nails at our sites.

He didn't have any hobbies. His work was consuming and he never tired of it, so diversions weren't necessary. He was always making notes, and at night and on weekends when he would talk on the phone, listening to him was an education all its own. He knew how to negotiate, and I think part of my strength as a negotiator comes from paying attention to him as he'd speak on the phone—which was always about his business. He was specific and didn't like to waste time. He'd get to the point immediately.

He also taught me to be wary. Through him, I learned that business requires toughness as well as insight. My father was such a hard worker that he could sense immediately if someone else wasn't. He was so solid that he could readily spot weakness in another person.

I also learned to trust my gut instinct. This can be developed, but it can also be an inherent talent. Sometimes I just don't feel right about a person. At other times, I know right away I like someone, which was the case with both Mark Burnett and Robert. I've had enough experience by now to know my instincts are well developed.

As an entrepreneur, you will have employees. I have a theory that every person you hire is a gamble, no matter what their credentials are. I've hired people from the best schools and they weren't so great. And I've hired people without credentials, and they were terrific. Sometimes it's the other way around. But it's not always easy to assess someone's abilities until you see them in action and give them a few challenges. I've been surprised, pleasantly and unpleasantly, over the years. But it's important to give people a chance to prove themselves.

With partners, it's a bit different. You can't count on much of a trial-and-error phase to assess a person's qualifications, so here's where the gut instinct comes in. It's difficult to explain how it works, but it's an unspoken dynamic that you must pay attention to. Partnerships must have loyalty and integrity at their core. Ask yourself if those two attributes make themselves apparent, and if they are working both ways. If a potential partner has to talk himself or herself up too much, that's sometimes a tip-off that something isn't quite right. Their level of confidence should be there to begin with. You want a partner, not an apprentice.

Partnerships also require negotiation. It should be a win–win setup. Otherwise, it's not a partnership. My criteria is that they have to be good people. I don't need to deal with any other kind of person.

Robert has had some tremendous learning experiences along the way, and his lessons are worth paying attention to. Even as entrepreneurs, we rely on people to get things done. We may have the original idea, but moving it forward can involve hundreds of people. Every person becomes integral to the overall success.

Partnerships Can Happen Quickly

I mentioned that I knew I liked Mark Burnett from the moment I met him, and that partnership has been thriving since 2003. *The Apprentice* premiered on television in January of 2004, and we've been going strong ever since. Mark knew I was new to the industry, and yet he showed great respect. We worked as collaborators from the start. He would listen to my suggestions and my questions (and I had a lot of them). He proved my first instinct was correct. He's a great person as well as a visionary.

Mark has had a great impact on the entertainment industry. One thing about him is that he never stops moving forward. He doesn't understand burnout and has very high quality controls for everything he does. We are not only co-producers, but we are friends and spend free time together. What most impressed me when I first met Mark was how direct he was. He had an idea, asked for a meeting, we made a deal and then we got to work. He knew exactly how *The Apprentice* should be presented on television and every detail was in place. He'd obviously given the idea a lot of thought, which made it much easier for me to make a decision. Convincing me wasn't that difficult when he was so thoroughly prepared. Obviously, he also had a successful background in television so I knew he was experienced and that he knew what he was talking about. He didn't have to hard-sell me, and the risk factor was definitely lessened.

Likewise, when I met Robert, I knew he was a good guy, and a smart one, too. I was impressed with his background story and the amazing number of books he has sold. I thought he'd be a great guy to write a book with, which was a good idea. He was my first collaborator. Our book was a big success and was just recently on the bestseller list in Shanghai again, which is saying something since it came out in 2006.

I am a fighter if people come after me. When people know you fight back, it makes them think twice about messing with you. That can save a lot of time and legal fees for everyone. I don't enjoy going after people, but sometimes it's necessary. I agree with Robert that success is the best revenge.

One thing that saved me from a lot of trial and error is the benefit I had from working with and watching my father from an early age. It was such a great education, and I remain grateful for his example. Robert didn't have that to the same extent in his life and he's learned some tough lessons—yet he's succeeded and credits his difficulties as his pathway to success. I've had my share of difficulties, but I think I learned to assess people from an early age due to my father's influence.

Learning to Manage a Team

When I was first starting out, I did a deal during college with my father in Cincinnati, Ohio. We found a federally financed housing foreclosure, Swifton Village, which was a 1,200-unit apartment development with 800 vacant apartments. It was in such a state of deterioration that no one else was bidding. It would be a big job, but we put in a minimal bid and it was accepted.

To make a long story short, within a year the place was beautifully refurbished and we had rented all the apartments. My point is that we had to go through about six different project managers before we found the right one. Some of the managers were honest, but not really bright. One of them actually painted himself into the corner of an apartment. I had to continually size them up and some just didn't have what it takes, like managerial smarts, for example. We eventually found the guy who would work out. He was actually a great bullshit artist and con man, but he had real talent as a manager. I could see he did a good job—most of the time. I just had to know how to handle him. I knew he wasn't completely trustworthy, so our relationship was one of guarded mutual respect. It wasn't ideal, but it worked for us, and Swifton Village did well under his care. He may have been a thief, but he was capable. I would joke with him and say, "We pay you $50,000 and all you can steal." It was an odd sort of negotiation, but he kept the place in good shape.

A number of years later, the neighborhood was turning bad, and we put the development up for sale. We got an immediate response. But working out the deal with this guy was a great lesson for me in negotiation and in partnership. For obvious reasons, my trust was limited, I was on guard, and that served me well.

My Teams

On any project we do, nationally and internationally, we will have teams on the job to handle the day-to-day necessities and demands that the site requires. Trump International Hotel & Tower Chicago will have a general manager, and so will every other project. Of course there will also be a full staff. In a way, these teams are very much like partnerships. All the entities have to work and flow together to be successful, particularly in the hotel industry, since it relies so heavily on superb service. Of course, that's a priority in all our buildings. My managers and all my employees know that I am demanding but fair, and the standard they represent can bring out the best in people.

I have a new team at The Trump Organization that has brought the Trump Hotel Collection to international recognition. The team I'm talking about is my three eldest children: Don, Ivanka, and Eric. They have worked on many projects and, as partners, they have proven themselves worthy. They may have started out as apprentices, but now that word only applies to their appearances as my advisors on *The Apprentice* TV show.

When I think of ideal partners, they are it. They work extremely hard, love what they do, and work independently with results that would make any good businessman proud. Ivanka has her own jewelry line as well as shoes and handbags, and she handles the extra responsibility like a pro. All three are active and effective with their charities, and their work ethic is beyond reproach. As a father, I couldn't be more proud. When it comes to three great partners, I'd say I'm a lucky man.

Bad Partner, Good Partner

Partners are crucial. For Robert, a good partner is, above all, trustworthy. Of course, they possess all the skills and talents necessary to be his partner, but honor for a Marine like Robert is at the top of the list. He only asks from others what he himself gives. And that's how you find a good partner. I look for people who have the same values as I do. It won't work otherwise.

If you question whether you would be a good partner, maybe you shouldn't be one. Not everyone is cut out for partnerships in the traditional sense. It's next to impossible to build a successful business without relationships. But you can do it without partners if you are capable of structuring deals and bringing in the right talent for specific projects or developments. For example, if I am building a new building, I will bring in the architect who will bring in his team, and I will find the right contractors, landscapers and so forth. It can be complex but worthwhile, because the entire development is yours and you're in control. So if you question whether or not you can build good business relationships, then I think it's time to look in the mirror and ask yourself why that is.

One way to become a good partner is to ask yourself, "What kind of partner would I like to have?" And then become that kind of partner yourself. Integrity has a way of attracting integrity, not that it will happen automatically. Some people aren't necessarily bad. They're just inept. Then again, some people are just plain bad. It's almost as if they can't help being that way. So I remain on guard until partners have proven themselves in a way that indicates they are solid.

I've had friends and partners who have become adversaries when it comes to a property. One friend went after exactly what he knew I was going after, and not in a partnership sort of way. It was a shock, since I'd known him a long time and considered him a friend. I'm happy to report that it all worked out, but it's something I learned from. I won't mention his name because it's unnecessary, but these things happen, and it was a good lesson. When it comes to business, people can be surprising, in every way.

On a recent episode of *The Celebrity Apprentice*, Niki Taylor was the project manager, and her team lost. Instead of looking for someone to blame, she took full responsibility for their loss and opened herself up to being fired. She displayed great integrity, and I admired her strength of character, as did her team. Her relationship to her team was one of complete respect, and she left with great dignity and admiration.

Deals vs. Partnerships

I remember having a conversation with Robert a few years ago about partnerships and how difficult they can be. He was in the middle of partnership woes. I prefer doing deals with other people, but not having partnerships because they are too complicated and can eventually go bad. Deals are easier. You still have the relationship, but not the baggage that a full partnership eventually requires. Partnerships are like marriage. They can be wonderful, or terrible. If you can, stick to doing deals with people you like and trust. Then you can move on from there to your next deal.

I've spent many years working on deals. My reputation is such that I can call in the right people, and we get things done easily. I understand that might not be so readily available to you, especially if you are just starting out, so I'd suggest that you keep the word "deal" in your head as you gradually move forward in your business career. Thinking "it's a deal" versus "it's a partnership" or "it's a marriage" is very freeing. Your mind will open up to new ideas. It's similar to my approach to difficult situations. I'll ask, "Is this a blip, or is it a catastrophe?" Most of the time it will fall into the blip category. It's amazing how much clearer things can be when you do that.

The Art of Negotiation

One skill you'll need to master is negotiation. I'm known for my negotiation skills and that comes with the territory of making deals. The best deals are good for everyone, which creates a win–win situation. Negotiation is persuasion more than power. It's a bit like diplomacy, although one can be a diplomat and still be stubborn. You've got to know what the other side wants and where they're coming from. Be reasonable and flexible, and never let anyone know exactly where you're coming from. Knowledge is power, so keep as much of it to yourself as possible. And remember the golden rule of negotiating: "He who has the gold makes the rules." That doesn't negate equal opportunity, but that's an unspoken fact that is definitely present. Always remember that you could be laying the groundwork for future business deals so the emphasis should be on fairness and integrity.

People like doing deals with me because they know it will be profitable, that I work quickly, and that they will be treated fairly. That's a reputation I've worked for, and it remains intact. It doesn't mean I'm easy, because I'm demanding. But I'm not confined by expectations and, more times than not, the deals work out to everyone's advantage. When Robert and I decided to write our first book together, it wasn't complicated. There was very little negotiation involved because it wasn't necessary.

I've had instances where I couldn't believe how much the other side didn't know. I immediately knew I could have a grand slam, and fast, just based on their apparent lack of information and preparation. That always astounds me. But I'm not out to slam-dunk anyone. It's just a good idea to be as prepared as possible with whatever you're doing. And sometimes it's good to play dumb. "It takes a lot of smarts to play dumb," as the saying goes. Why? It's a good way to see how much your negotiating partners don't know. It's also a good way to see if they are bulldozing you. Bottom line: Trust your instincts, especially if they are well honed.

New entrepreneurs might ask, "How do you hone your instincts?" That comes with experience, but I think we all have that inner buzzer that goes off. Heed it. You may not even be able to verbalize it, but it will serve as a warning. I've often advised people to "be paranoid." That's a way of saying to be wary. Another way is to make sure you're prepared every day. Make use of the media to be aware of global and national events. Work at being well versed on as many topics and industries as possible.

Criticism and Conflict

I've had relationships with the media that go from the best to the worst. The good ones last. I've done many television interviews with Regis Philbin, Barbara Walters, Larry King, Neil Cavuto, *Access Hollywood*, and many others over the years. I'm a frequent guest, and we maintain professional relationships, and sometimes friendships, because the respect goes both ways. There's professional and personal rapport.

But on occasion over the years, I've been skewered by the press—in fact, on many occasions. But the fact remains that there are a lot of great writers and journalists who can and will be fair.

I can remember being criticized when Trump World Tower at United Nations Plaza went up. An article appeared in *The New York Times* by the esteemed architecture critic Herbert Muschamp, who praised it as "a handsome hunk of a glass tower." He then commented that "Trump does better when he ignores his critics than when he pays attention to them." Criticism is easier to take when you realize that the only people who aren't criticized are those who don't take risks. Don't be afraid of the risk involved—and know you're in good company if you're criticized.

People will target you if it will bring attention to themselves. There's usually a subtext to their attack, which is something I realized after being targeted multiple times. One way to fizzle their fire is not to respond, because they're just trying to get a reaction from you. In the meantime, they've brought attention to you, and that can work for you in some cases. Be sure to view both sides when and if this happens to you, because there are times when a response of self-defense is warranted.

I've also been involved in a lot of lawsuits, which aren't my favorite thing, but sometimes they're just plain necessary. People step out of line and become unreasonable or unscrupulous. You have to deal with them, or you'll be known as a pushover. You have to stand up for yourself.

"Business is easy. People are difficult," as Robert's rich dad said. But people skills come with experience and attentiveness. And like Robert, I've had some tremendous people in my life who are solid gold, and their backgrounds, experiences and professions are as diverse as can be. Many of them have become friends as a result of deals we've done. So from day one of your business life, take into account the importance of your partnerships—on both a personal and professional level.

Distilling It Down: Relationships

Business is easy. Dealing with people is hard. There is a saying that goes, "You cannot choose your family, but you can choose your friends." If you are an employee, you cannot choose your fellow employees. But if you are an entrepreneur, your most important job is to choose who works with you. In fact, there is no job that is more important, because your employees are the ones who will represent you and your company.

Your Personal Development Program

Becoming an entrepreneur can be the best personal-development program you can enter, and your business can be your best business school. If you grow personally, your business will grow. Unfortunately, if you don't grow personally, the opposite is also true.

Entrepreneurship is like the game of golf. When you miss that five-foot putt, there's no one else to blame except yourself, no matter how hard you try to find another reason.

Although other people's actions can affect your bottom line, the bottom line is that it's *your* bottom line. When other people lose your business's money, it's still your business and your money. If your advisors give you bad advice, you pay for that bad advice, in amounts far greater than simply the fee you paid. If you blame others for your losses, you lose more than money. You lose an opportunity to learn, grow, and become a better entrepreneur.

One reason why most people stay in the E quadrant or stay very small in the S quadrant is because they do not want to take responsibility for other people. People can be your greatest asset, or your greatest liability.

Your Most Important Job

One reason many people do not do well in business is because they do not do well with people. Do you know anyone like that? A person who just can't relate to people? He or she might be a great engineer, accountant, inventor, attorney, artist, or singer, but just can't get along with people. The Midas Touch is really about you and your relationship to people. Working well with people is your most important job, and it isn't easy. Why? Because people come in a lot of different shapes, sizes and flavors. Here are some of the people you will need to relate to as an entrepreneur.

Working with Investors

These are the people who have the power to turn your idea into a business. If they lack faith in your entrepreneurial skills, they'll say, "Great idea—but no thank you." They may not say it that nicely, however. Ironically, the world is filled with investors looking for great investments. The problem is that there are very few great entrepreneurs who are worth investing in. Your job is to become a great entrepreneur who is worth investing in. That takes personal growth, because being an entrepreneur is very different from being an employee. An entrepreneur must have skills most people don't have.

Here's your first lesson on raising money. Let's call it "Raising Money 101." First of all, most people have great ideas. The problem is that they cannot raise money because they are looking at the whole exercise from the wrong side of the desk. If you want to raise money, you need to look at the world through the eyes of a professional investor in the I quadrant. Professional investors don't really care about your product, although products do matter. The first thing the professional investor wants to know is: who you are, your experience, your team, and who else stands behind you. They want to know who you have as your partners, your advisory board, your banker, and other investors. A pro looks at the people, because they know business is about people.

Since most new entrepreneurs have no experience as entrepreneurs, and professional entrepreneurs will not invest in them or their business, many start-up businesses raise money from friends and family, betting on friendship and love rather than on business skills. This is where it all gets tricky. It's a catch-22. You want a chance to prove you're an entrepreneur with great business skills, but you have to convince people that you are an entrepreneur before you can acquire the great business skills. This is precisely why the next type of person is important.

Working with Partners

Some entrepreneurs are solo acts, but many others have partners. Partners are important because no one can know all the answers or possess all the skills required at every level of the B-I Triangle. Having a partner can increase your chance of surviving your first five years, the time period when most new businesses fail.

The best partnerships are the ones where each person brings complementary skills, talents, and experiences to the company. For example, it's common to see one partner who is outgoing and the other who excels inside the business operations. In other partnerships, you might find one partner who loves the big picture and another who loves detail. You get the idea. A business partnership is like a marriage. If you choose the right partner, it can be heaven. Choose the wrong partner, and it will be hell.

The best partnerships are made up of three different people:

1. **The Dreamer**

    This person has the pretty picture, the perfect vision of a beautiful future.

2. **The Business Person**

    This person runs the business. The business person makes sure the pieces of the puzzle fit, and the trains run on time.

3. **The S.O.B.**

    This is the guard dog. They trust no one and don't believe anyone. If someone needs to be bitten, this is the person you call upon to do it.

We have learned to become all three people. Some entrepreneurs are only one or two. Are you able to be all three? If not, hire the person or persons you're not, because you will need all three.

Here's some cheap but effective legal advice. Before becoming an official partner in a business, it is best to have an attorney draw up a "buy-sell" agreement, just in case things go bad or one partner wants to keep the business and the other wants to move on. A buy-sell agreement is like a pre-nuptial before the wedding. As you know, most wedding ceremonies end with the line, "Till death do us part." One reason why 50 percent of most marriages end in divorce is because divorce is much better than death.

Like many couples, many potential partnerships find out they are incompatible when they begin working on their buy-sell agreement. The same is true with a pre-nuptial agreement. It is best to find out your differences early, rather than after the business or marriage begins.

There is an old joke that goes like this:

Therapist: "Why do you have so many relationship problems?"

Client: "I seem to attract the wrong kind of men."

Therapist: "That's not true. Your problems begin when you give them your phone number."

Be careful when choosing partners. As they say, "Falling in love is easy. Staying in love is hard." The problems begin once the honeymoon is over. If you cannot solve problems together, the problems only pile up. In marriage and in business, it is easy to hate the people you once loved.

So start with a buy-sell before becoming partners. We all have good sides and bad sides. Simply discussing a buy-sell may allow you to see your potential partner's real side, and your own.

Only dreamers think relationships are always happy. All relationships have disagreements. If you have good partners, your disagreements can be productive. Many times, better ideas come out of heated discussions. However, if there are only arguments, fights, disagreements, and no better ideas that come from it all, the partnership is a bad partnership. When Larry Page and Sergey Brin first met, they disagreed on almost everything. Then they agreed on Google.

How to Be a Good Partner

You may notice on *The Apprentice* that Donald listens, watches, and asks questions more than he talks or bestows advice. This is what good leaders do. Our creator gave us two eyes, two ears, and only one mouth. The message is: Listen more, observe more, and talk less. If people are only talking and no one is listening, the business has very big problems. Leaders who talk, but fail to listen, are not good leaders.

When asking an investor for money, it is best to speak less and listen more. You will learn a lot about business by knowing what investors think is important.

Working with Advisors

Investors want to know who your advisors are. All public companies are required to have a board of directors. Even if you are not planning to take your business public, you should have a board of advisors. For example, if you are planning on starting a restaurant, you should have advisors who have successfully started and operated a restaurant. You also need good legal and accounting advisors. Take your time choosing your advisors. Not all advisors are good advisors. Your advisory board can save you a lot of time, heartache, and money. A professional investor will be looking at your advisors and their credentials.

Think of advisors as your business school instructors and your best teachers. Having a real business and a team of real-world advisors can be the best way to gain a real-world business education. But you have to do your part, and that means being a good student, listening, learning, and making corrections. You do not have to do everything your advisors tell you to do, but you do have to listen to everything they tell you. If you do not listen, you do not need advisors, or you need to change advisors.

Working with Your Employees

This is often the toughest group you will work with, but hang in there because your employees can be your best teachers. Since a business is made up of different skills (skills such as accounting, legal, customer service, marketing, advertising, sales, product development, and more) represented by the 8 Integrities of Business, you are dealing with a group of highly specialized people. Some will be motivated, some not, some honest, some not. Getting this group to focus on the objectives of the business is no easy task, but it is your task. Remember, one bad apple will ruin the other apples. It is important to learn how to protect your workers from bad apples. If an investor senses you have employee problems or you are not a competent leader, they will not invest in you.

One of the biggest complaints you'll either use yourself or hear from other entrepreneurs is, "I can't find good people." Since most new entrepreneurs have little real-world experience leading people, they often say, "You can't find good workers these days." In most cases, the real problem is that the entrepreneur is not yet a good leader. As entrepreneurs develop their leadership skills, their employees will improve.

Working with Your Customers

Last but not least, a business must have customers and great customer relationships. Your customers will be some of your best teachers.

A professional investor will always ask, "Who is the customer, and why do they need your product or service?" In a world of ever-increasing competition for your customer's time and money, you must know your customer, why your customer needs your business, and how you stay in a relationship with them.

Often, entrepreneurs in the S quadrant have a one-to-one relationship with their customers. Some examples would be the doctor–patient relationship in medicine and the attorney–client relationship in law.

In the B quadrant, the relationship is different. It is no longer one-to-one. B-quadrant entrepreneurs must keep a person-to-person relationship via different media, which again requires different skills.

We maintain a person-to-person relationship with our millions of customers via our management teams, TV, radio, social media, personal appearances, and books. Obviously, an investor wants to know how you will attract and keep good customers.

The Best Business School

This is why your business can be your best business school and a personal-development program that lasts forever. If you get better, everything else gets better. If you become great, money and fame pour in. And if you blame, remember that the word "blame" means "be lame." The world is filled with lame entrepreneurs, often because they fail to see their business as their business school.

Quick Pitch

Are you ready for your quick pitch? You'll need it because it is critical to raising money. First, you must know what to say, and this is where branding and planning come into play. But once you've honed your words, it's time to practice, practice practice.

Like anything in life, if you want to be good, you must practice. Learn to pitch your business quickly. The better you get at pitching, the better you and your business get.

Remember the thumb. The thumb builds your strength of character. Your index finger keeps you focused during the pitch. Your middle finger reminds you of your brand and what you stand for. And your ring finger reminds you to build better relationships. So practice pitching. The more you pitch, the more you learn and the better you become. The better you are, the better your relationships.

They call it a quick pitch because it must be short and sweet. Like most of us, investors are busy people and they will have no time and little patience for long, boring sales pitches. Get to the point, and get to the point quickly.

Guide to the Quick Pitch

A simple guide to pitching your investment focuses on four main points. Interestingly, these are the same four points you should follow when designing your business. Allow no more than two minutes to pitch each of the four points.

1. **Project**
   - What is the project?
   - Why is it unique?
   - Why is the business needed?
   - Why will customers love your product?

2. **Partners**
   - Who are you?
   - Who are the partners?
   - What are your educational backgrounds?
   - How much experience do you all have?
   - How are you and your partners qualified to make the project a success?

3. **Financing**
   - What is the total cost of the project?
   - How much debt and how much equity is there?
   - Are partners investing their own money?
   - What is the investor's return and reward for their risk?
   - What are the tax consequences?
   - Who is your CFO or accounting firm?
   - Who is responsible for investor communications?
   - What is the investor's exit?

4. **Management**
   - Who is running your company?
   - What is their experience?
   - What is their track record?
   - Have they ever failed?
   - How does their experience relate to your industry?
   - Do you believe this is the strongest management team you can assemble?
   - Can you pitch them with confidence?

This is your pitch, with a total time of eight minutes or less. Once you have briefly covered the four points, shut up. Ask for questions, listen, and respond with brief answers. Remember to ask questions more than give answers.

You should also be asking questions of the potential investor, questions such as:

- Does this project interest you?
- Have you ever invested in a start-up project?
- What are your concerns?

If, and only if, they are really interested, then break out the business plan and other relevant information. Remember, the person who talks the most, loses. The person who listens the most, wins.

Listening is a sign of respect. Being interested rather than trying to be interesting is also a sign of respect. Be respectful, and you will win, not only in business, but in life.

Two Tips on Raising Money

Tip #1: Seek advice from accountants and attorneys when preparing your pitch.

Not only is it good practice, it is fabulous education. If they are sharp accountants and attorneys, you will be forming great relationships. They can also introduce you to other great people.

If they are incompetent professionals, and there are many of them, you and your business will suffer. So take your time and be picky when selecting attorneys and accountants.

Tip #2: Begin asking for money before you need the money.

All you need to say is, "I'm starting a business in a few months." Briefly describe the business, and why you're excited about it. This pitch should take less than a minute. Again, if you keep talking, you lose. After a minute, ask questions such as, "Are you interested? Would you like to hear more?" If the answer is yes, then ask, "May I call you when we are ready to start talking to potential investors?"

If they say yes, take their name and keep your promise to call them—in the future, not the next day.

Remember the rule: "It is easier to ask for money when you don't need the money." You don't ever want to sound desperate and needy, even if you are. Don't give them sob stories or tales of woe. Avoid exaggeration and promises of excessive returns. Investors are more likely to believe someone who is conservative and cautious, rather than excessive and cocky. So start early, practice, don't over-promise, and obey these rules for raising capital.

What Investors Are Afraid Of

Many people dream of quitting their job and starting their own business, but they are afraid of failing. This is a legitimate concern.

Yet, becoming an entrepreneur is no big deal. Almost anyone can become one. For example, if a young boy or girl mows their neighbor's lawn for $10, he or she is an entrepreneur.

What determines if that boy or girl becomes a great entrepreneur is what they do with that money.

Many entrepreneurs simply stick the $10 in their pocket. Millions of small entrepreneurs around the world do this. When they stick the money in their pocket, they join the underground economy, keeping no records and paying no taxes.

This is what most professional investors are afraid of. They know most small entrepreneurs stick the money in their pocket, feeding themselves rather than feeding the business and returning the investors' money. On top of that, stuffing money in your own pocket is a criminal act. Most investors do not invest with criminals.

The world is filled with S-quadrant entrepreneurs who are tax cheats and criminals, members of the underground economy. You come across these entrepreneurs at swap meets, garage sales, farmer's markets, people cleaning houses on weekends, people washing your car window while you wait for the light to change, waiters and bartenders not declaring their tips, and billions of other people doing anything they can to make a buck. In the United States alone, the underground economy is estimated to be a $1.5 to $2 trillion economy and growing. Without records, it is difficult to measure this economy.

If you are in this record-less and tax-less economy, it is best to stay small and under the radar. The problem with being in the underground economy is becoming rich. If a person in the underground makes a lot of money, suddenly buying a big house, driving flashy cars, sailing their new boat, and charging large sums on their credit cards, their "living large" puts them on the radar screen of the tax department. If caught for tax evasion, their business is often destroyed and they will spend a lot of time and money defending themselves.

Obviously, we do not recommend becoming entrepreneurs in the underground economy. We mention the underground economy simply to acknowledge it exists and is thriving, and to advise you to avoid it if you want the Midas Touch.

From E to S

Employees do not need to keep records and pay taxes. The company they work for does that for them. If they do prepare taxes, it is primarily for a tax refund. Employees do not need a CPA or tax attorney because there is little these professionals can do for an employee. There are very few tax breaks for employees. To make matters worse, the more money an employee makes, the more taxes they pay.

It is this lack of knowledge about taxes and records that gets even honest entrepreneurs in trouble. When a person moves from the E quadrant into the S quadrant, they run into a flurry of taxes and government regulations few employees know about. This is why relationships with professionals like accountants and tax advisors are so important.

Entrepreneurs face additional taxes such as:

- Sales tax

- Self-employment tax

- FICA (Federal Income Compensation Act, aka Social Security and Medicare)

- State unemployment tax

- Federal unemployment tax

- Other taxes and regulations

We can better understand the problem with taxes using the example of a kid earning $10. An employee in the E quadrant earning $10 will pay approximately 30 percent in taxes, netting seven dollars.

A self-employed person in the S quadrant earning $10 will pay approximately 60 percent in taxes, netting four dollars. This is why most small entrepreneurs simply put the $10 in their pocket, becoming tax cheats and criminals. This is what many investors are afraid of.

High Unemployment

This example also illustrates why unemployment is so high. Why would anyone want to become an entrepreneur when the government punishes the small entrepreneur with more taxes and excessive rules and regulations? Why take all that risk only to be punished by the government? How can a small entrepreneur survive when the government is your biggest expense? How can an entrepreneur hire new employees when the government makes hiring employees more and more expensive? If you are unemployed, why become an entrepreneur if you can make more money collecting free money from the government?

The problem is the solution. In other words, taxes and regulations are the problem, and also the way out of the problem. One of the best advantages of becoming an entrepreneur is that the government gives you a tax break for accounting, legal, and tax advice. Employees are not allowed this tax break. If an employee hires an accountant, they pay for that advice with after-tax dollars. As an entrepreneur, you pay for this advice with pre-tax dollars. In simple terms, the government gives you a tax break for hiring smart advisors. This is where the entrepreneur gets their real-world education that employees never receive.

Most small entrepreneurs see taxes, accountants, and attorneys as parasites. Yet, with a change in their point of view, an entrepreneur may see taxes, accounts, and attorneys as their partners in developing their Midas Touch. The problem with most S's is that they are former E's who quit their jobs and now *own* their jobs. They do not own a business. The tax laws are written for people who own businesses, not for people who own jobs.

The most important job of an S is to turn their job into a business. They do that by developing their Midas Touch and evolving into the B and I quadrants.

How Does an S Become a B?

The irony is that tax laws are really incentives and stimulus laws. The tax laws are encouraging all of us to become B's and I's. At the same time, the tax laws punish those in the E and S quadrants. This is true all over the world.

Most entrepreneurs in the S quadrant are so busy keeping their job, they fail to do their real job, which is to grow their business into the B and I quadrants. If you do not do your real job, the government will punish you with excessive taxes.

Why Are Taxes Incentives?

Tax breaks are given to people who do what the government wants done. That includes things like:

1. Creating jobs
2. Producing food
3. Providing housing
4. Providing energy

If you want to know more about taxes, hire an accountant or tax attorney and ask them about the four points listed above. If they tell you these tax breaks cannot be done, or it is too risky, look for smarter advisors who are willing to educate you, not just charge you by the hour. Taxes are so critical. That's why we're talking about them here. But you can't take advantage of your rights unless you have solid relationships with excellent advisors.

Once you understand taxes in the B and I quadrants, you will know why companies such as General Electric make billions of dollars and pay virtually nothing in taxes, legally. They have great advisors that the government helps the business pay for.

This is also why governments bail out big banks and big businesses and then increases taxes on E's and S's. Taxes are revenue-neutral. That means if the government gives, it must also take. So it gives tax breaks to those who are doing what the government wants done, and takes taxes from those who are not doing what the government wants done.

The job of an entrepreneur is to move from E to S, then S to B, and raise capital from the I quadrant. The government wants the same thing. The process looks like this:

This is the path of most great entrepreneurs.

- Henry Ford started Ford Motor Company in his garage.
- Michael Dell started Dell computers in his college dorm room.
- Steve Jobs started Apple in a garage.
- Sergey Brin and Larry Page started Google in college.
- Mark Zuckerberg started Facebook in college.
- Hewlett and Packard started their technology company in a garage.
- Bill Gates purchased his Microsoft operating system from a small programming company.

Then they made their way through the CASHFLOW Quadrant.

A Final Thought

A big difference between S-quadrant entrepreneurs and B-quadrant entrepreneurs is the word "network." Most E's and S's are not aware of the power of networks, but the richest people and biggest businesses actually own networks. This is why the rich own television networks, radio networks, franchise networks, network-marketing businesses, and broker/dealer networks.

The good news is that technology makes it easier than ever before to build networks and keep networks connected. Technology makes it easier to evolve into the B and I quadrants. Today, businesses are doing business worldwide in an instant. That is why there are so many young millionaires and billionaires in their twenties.

Although technology makes it easier, entrepreneurs still need great relationships to advise, guide, and help them grow into the B and I quadrants. For entrepreneurs to attract better people, entrepreneurs must become people of better legal, ethical, and moral character. They must become smarter too.

Even if you have very little money, not much real-world business experience, and few friends who are entrepreneurs, look at your business as your own personal business school and personal-development program. There is much to know. Your relationships are your instructors. The more you grow, the more your business grows.

Points to Remember | Things to Do

- Not everyone is cut out to be a partner and not everyone needs a partner. But partners that have different skills from yours can be very valuable.

- Partners won't always agree. But if you don't come out of disagreements with a better idea, the partnership might be a bad one.

- There are many types of people you will have to work with. Approach them from their needs, not your own.

- You'll need investors to grow. Part of developing solid relationships is respecting their time, their attention and getting right to the point with a quick pitch.

- Taxes are a big issue as you move from E to S, and then from S to B and I. Do not overlook this important aspect of business management. Develop relationships with the best tax advisors you can find.

- In the end, the more you grow through the people you surround yourself with, the more your business will grow. Be picky.

- Partner with people who share your values, attitude and drive.

- Plan for the end of the partnership before you begin it by drawing up a buy-sell agreement. You may find that you are incompatible even before you sign it. That would be a good thing.

THE LITTLE FINGER
LITTLE THINGS THAT COUNT

"If we did all the things we are capable of,
we would literally astound ourselves."

— Thomas Edison

Little Things Are Big Things
Robert Kiyosaki

First of all, there is a big difference between *little things that count* and *thinking small*. It is a big reason why so few entrepreneurs develop their Midas Touch. Too many entrepreneurs *think small* and fail to focus on *the little things that count*.

The CASHFLOW Quadrant

Let's start with the basics. I always come back to the CASHFLOW Quadrant because it clearly explains so many aspects of business behavior. It makes it easier to understand why so many entrepreneurs are trapped in small thinking. It's not their fault. They just happen to be living in the context of the E and S quadrants.

Employees (E's) may quit their jobs and start their own small business. In other words, they migrate to the S quadrant. Nothing wrong with that, except that most of them stay there. The S, as you'll recall, stands for small and specialized, and that's what these businesses are. The problem is that S can also stand for struggle, and sometimes selfish.

Many people in the S quadrant are happy there and that is fine. But many would love to migrate to the B quadrant, the realm of business, and to the I quadrant, the realm of the investor. Both of those quadrants represent freedom and infinite wealth. They are the quadrants of the rich.

It's not that E's and S's aren't smart enough to move to the B and I quadrants. Often they are too smart for their own good. It's their small thinking that keeps them trapped in the S quadrant. And yes, I mean trapped. S's often work harder than anyone else.

Here are few examples of their small thinking.

Example #1: Working hard, but thinking small

I have a friend who owns a small restaurant. He has been in business for years. Every morning before the sun comes up, my friend goes down to the produce markets to shop for the freshest fruits, vegetables, meats, poultry, and fish. By 9:00 a.m., he's back in his restaurant preparing for the lunch crowd. At 10:30 a.m. his two waitresses come in and begin setting up the dining room. By 11:00 a.m. he is open for business. He is busy through lunch, personally coming out of the kitchen to greet his customers. He finally has a break around 2:00 p.m. While his dishwashers clean, he goes home to take a short nap. He returns around 5:00 p.m. to prepare for the dinner crowd. He is in bed by 11:00 p.m., ready to begin the next day. He does this six days a week.

He complains about the long hours, taxes, rising food costs, government regulations, and the struggle to find and keep good employees. He is also upset because none of his five children wants to take over the business.

He believes it is his personal touch—selecting the ingredients, greeting every customer that comes in, his white tablecloths, generous drinks, and fair prices—that keeps his customers coming back. And he may be right.

But it's also his small thinking that keeps him working long hours and his earnings low. What he thinks are *the little things that count* are really an example of *thinking small.*

My friend is not poor. He makes enough money. But he's doubtful that his business will ever grow or attain much wealth. I know that it won't unless he stops thinking small and begins thinking about the little things that count.

Example #2: Thinking small, and getting smaller

I have another friend who is a very successful real estate agent. When the real estate market crashed in 2007, so did her business. Rather than change her thinking, she chose to close her office, let most of her staff go, and work from home. She downsized, just like the economy.

At a recent party, she came up to me and asked, "Have you lost your real estate investments?"

"No," I replied with a smile. "In fact, 2010 has been the best year of my life. Kim and I have purchased five large apartment houses for a total of nearly 1,400 new rental units, including a resort hotel and five golf courses for about $87 million."

"Why didn't you call me if you were looking for investments?" she asked in surprise. "You know I sell real estate. I'm still in business."

"Why didn't you call me?" I replied. "You know I invest in real estate."

"I just assumed the real estate market was bad and no one was buying," she grumbled back at me. "How did you get the loans? How did you find the money for the down payments?"

With that response, it was clear that we were talking across a great divide. For her, her real estate business was struggling and for me, my real estate business was booming. At the end of the evening, she made one more attempt to connect, saying,
"Call me the next time you want to buy something."

I replied, "Call me when you find something."

So far, she has not called.

Example #3: A specialized specialist
A very smart classmate of mine went on to medical school to become a highly specialized doctor. It was a long, long process. He became a highly specialized small specialist in the S quadrant.

About three years ago, he was diagnosed with stomach cancer and had to stop practicing medicine. Immediately, his lifestyle changed and his income plummeted. The good news is that he recovered and is back to rebuilding his practice and his patient base. The problem is that he is physically weaker and unable to work the long hours he once did. Hence, his income remains low.

He wants to retire but, without seeing patients, he has no way to earn enough money to cover his everyday expenses, much less his retirement. He plans on working for the rest of his life, but does not know how much life he has left.

These three entrepreneurs are examples of successful people trapped in the S quadrant, thinking small and failing to do the little things that count.

What Are the Little Things?

The little things that count is a concept also known as a competitive edge in business. It is something unique that the entrepreneur has and brings to the business, not just in the S quadrant, but also in the B and I quadrants.

Now I can hear some of you saying, "But the restaurant owner, the real estate agent, and the doctor all had a specialty. They were doing the little things, but the little things did not count."

This is true, but here is the subtle difference: The little things that counted were their personal specialties, not their business specialties. Until the little thing that you do becomes the little thing that the business does, it will not count. Until my friends' specialties became their business' specialties, they would remain trapped in the S quadrant. In their cases, it was their specialties, things only they could do, that kept them small.

Here are few examples of little things that count.

Little Thing #1: Faster pizza

Pizza is one of the most popular foods in America and the world. Almost every town in America has a pizza parlor, and every grocery store carries frozen pizza. It's hard to pick up your mail and not find a "two-pizza deal" coupon in some circular. It's a highly competitive business, crowded with competitors on every corner.

Decades ago, Domino's Pizza burst onto the crowded pizza scene with "pizza in 30 minutes or less." A pizza in 30 minutes or less is an example of a little thing that counts. Domino's was aware that, when people get hungry for a pizza, they don't want to wait. So in 1973, Domino's redesigned their entire business in the B quadrant around this 30-minute promise. Their already-successful business boomed. Thirty minutes is not a big thing. But for Domino's, it was the little thing that made a big difference.

Unfortunately, in their haste to keep their 30-minute promise, there were two accidents involving delivery vehicles. Domino's was sued for millions and has since dropped the promise. Nonetheless, when I think of ordering pizza, Domino's 30-minute promise still comes to mind, even though they no longer guarantee it.

Domino's 30-minute promise is an example of a little thing that counted. It was a promise that an entire business in the B quadrant was built around. Today, Domino's has locations in over 60 countries. Thirty minutes or not, they still sell a lot of pizzas.

Little Thing #2: Always low prices

Walmart, the biggest employer in America, built a business around one little thing that customers want—low prices. Sam Walton, founder of Walmart, did not just cut or discount some prices. As he grew from the S quadrant to the B quadrant, he built the entire business around that one simple brand promise—low prices. Low prices are the DNA of Walmart's enormous and complex business focused on delivering the lowest prices on great products. Walmart's business—the warehouses, trucking, purchasing, computer systems, everything—is focused on keeping their promise to deliver low prices, always.

Recently, during the financial crisis that started in 2007, many businesses were forced to cut their prices just to get people into their stores. Unfortunately, because some retail businesses were not designed to deliver low prices, the price cuts put them out of business.

Across the world, millions of small businesses are driven out of business simply because they cannot compete with the likes of Walmart, Home Depot, and low-cost online businesses like Amazon. The little things that count make a business big.

Now that you understand how entrepreneurs keep businesses small by thinking and acting small, here is how it looks from the business perspective. We'll use the B-I Triangle.

The entire B-I Triangle is focused on the little things. The DNA of the business begins with the mission of the business, the base. Once Sam Walton was clear on his mission to give his customers the lowest prices possible, he found his life's mission and built the rest of the business to fulfill that mission.

When S-quadrant people cut their prices or discount their services, they often fail because they only cut the price of their product. The rest of the business doesn't change. The other areas of the B-I Triangle keep on doing what they were doing before. That won't work. A company built for higher prices will die when prices are lowered too far, unless everything else changes accordingly.

Little Thing #3: Overnight shipping
Federal Express, now called FedEx, burst onto the business scene with the promise of overnight shipping. Overnight was a little thing that counted big. Today, FedEx is a multibillion-dollar business.

Because of its worldwide operations, FedEx had to drop the positively overnight guarantee. Nonetheless, overnight remains in the DNA, the mission of FedEx.

Little Thing #4: You deserve a break today

McDonald's knows what it feels like to be a parent with small kids. Keeping kids happy is another little thing that counts. I have never seen an unhappy kid at McDonald's. And I have seen a lot of relieved parents who are happy their kids are happy.

Whenever I hear nutritionists rant about how bad McDonald's food is for kids, I know that nutritionist does not get why McDonald's is so successful. A trip to McDonald's has nothing to do with food. A trip to McDonald's is all about happy kids and parents who need a break. To recite McDonald's latest campaign: "I'm lovin' it."

Taking another look at the B-I Triangle, you get a glimpse into the brilliance of McDonald's global systems.

When a person steps up to a McDonald's counter and says, "I want a Big Mac, medium fries, and a Coke," the entire B-I Triangle goes into hyper-efficiency. Immediately, the burger, fries, and Coke, the *product* in the B-I Triangle, come together from sources all over the world. They are delivered to you in less than five minutes. If that is not a miracle, I do not know what is. On top of that, the precision and efficiency is duplicated worldwide, in cities and towns everywhere. That's *systems* in the B-I Triangle.

Actually, if you ever want to understand the power of the B-I Triangle, simply go to the McDonald's nearest you and sit there for an hour. Imagine the millions of workers it takes to keep the B-I Triangle functioning—delivering what customers want, what keeps kids happy and parents relieved—in less than five minutes, all over the world. One person, an S, cannot do it. It takes millions of people.

I marvel at this. The moment you place your order, buns from the wheat fields and bakeries throughout the world are in action. Tons of potatoes are cut and ready for deep-frying. Beef from all over the world is butchered, ground, formed into patties, and ready when you want it. The Coke is bubbly, sharp, and crisp. The taste is consistent, and the bathrooms are clean. McDonald's is an excellent example of an efficient, global B-quadrant business that knows its customers. That little thing is a big thing. They know what their customers want.

Donald understands what I'm talking about with all these examples. He has been true to the little thing that is a big thing when it comes to his business. When people stay at a Trump hotel, purchase a Trump property, or play 18 holes on a Trump golf course, they are buying the money, sex, fame, and power of Trump. That is Donald's brand. That is his promise. That is the little thing he does that makes the big difference. He turns them into big things, very big things. It all matters to his customers and it all works together.

Little Thing #5: Simple and fun

The little thing that counts for Rich Dad is that we keep financial education simple and fun. Many people freeze up whenever there is talk about money, finance, or even numbers. Most of Rich Dad's competitors are too serious and boring. They act like dictators, shaking their finger at you saying, "Cut up your credit cards, save money, and live below your means." They treat people like children, telling them what to do and not trying to truly educate them.

They say you're supposed to live below your means. Easy to say, but who wants to settle for less? I don't. You don't. In my opinion, living below your means kills your spirit. I think most people are like me. They'd rather expand their means than live below it.

Also, after this last financial crisis, many people now know that my competitors' financial advice is bad advice. Rather than make them rich, people who followed my competitors' advice lost a lot of money. Now they are giving advice on how to recover and advice on what to do now. I can't figure out what their little thing is that is a big thing, but I know Rich Dad's little thing is—financial education that is simple and fun.

People wondered why Donald and I teamed up in 2006 to write our first book, *Why We Want You To Be Rich*. We did it because we both were seeing a looming problem: the disappearing middle class. We warned people in that book. We put it all in simple terms. We wanted people to be rich because we didn't want them to end up poor. As the middle class disappears, there's only one of two ways you can go: rich or poor. We want you to be rich. That's also why this book is important. We're putting in simple terms how you can build a successful Midas Touch business so you don't end up like my friends—the restaurant owner, the real estate agent, and the doctor.

Little Thing #6: Have fun learning

When I was about nine years old, my rich dad began teaching his son and me about money using the game of *Monopoly*. In other words, rich dad made learning fun, challenging, and interesting. Today, I am a rich man because I had fun playing *Monopoly* as a kid.

In 1984, the year I decided to stop being a manufacturer of wallets, I became a teacher who taught business, investing, and entrepreneurship using many different games. Kim and I spent 10 years becoming pretty good at using games as educational tools.

In 1996, before there was a *Rich Dad Poor Dad* book, we launched our game *CASHFLOW 101*. Today, that game is played all over the world in about 15 languages.

It is successful because people have fun learning about finances with play money. Once they play the game, many go on to learn about more financial subjects they are interested in.

There are now board games and online games for *CASHFLOW 101* and the advanced *CASHFLOW 202* as well as games for kids. There are free or low-cost *CASHFLOW* game challenges all over the world. Using games helps us keep a complex and boring subject simple and fun. Simple and fun is Rich Dad's little thing that counts.

Two Lessons from Military School

As you now know, Donald and I both went to military schools. He attended the New York Military Academy, and I attended the U.S. Merchant Marine Academy, also in New York. I believe military schools give us both an unfair advantage in the world of business.

Unlike traditional schools, there is a strong emphasis in military schools on mission, leadership skills, team skills, courage, focus and discipline. The following two lessons from the academy have served me well in business.

Lesson #1: The difference between tactics and strategies

Tactics are what you do. In very simple terms, a leader must define the single tactic, the single objective of the team or organization.

All strategies are in support of ensuring that the single tactic, the objective, is accomplished.

Businesses begin to fail when they have too many tactics and too many strategies. You'll get what I'm talking about when you see the following diagram of a successful military campaign.

Using Domino's Pizza as an example (the pizza with the 30-minutes-or-less promise), all the company's strategies—advertising strategies, legal strategies, accounting strategies, product-development strategies—are clearly encompassed within the B-I Triangle. All these strategies must support the single tactic, the focus of the business, the promise to the customer.

Problems arise in organizations when strategies become more important than the singular unifying tactic.

I have seen this happen many times. Attorneys may think legal documents are more important than the customer. Or human resources staff may hire people that may have all the qualifications but don't fit the culture of the business. Or accounting, in the name of doing things right, doesn't transform their systems to keep up with the speed of the transactions.

When strategies break down, solving them takes time, money, and focus away from the core tactic. Sales fall, expenses go up, and profits suffer. The lesson is that not one of the business integrities within the B-I Triangle is more important than any of the others.

This leads to the second lesson from military school.

Lesson #2: The leader's job is to unite and focus the entire B-I Triangle.
Most of us are familiar with the phrase "Divide and conquer." That's what our traditional education system is built upon. From the moment a child starts school, the educational system begins dividing kids into smart, average and, today what they call, under-performing (although when I was in school we were called stupid). This dividing and conquering is training kids for life in the E and S quadrants.

In the E and S quadrants, life is about competing for a job or promotions or pay-raises. This dividing-to-conqueror programming is why many E's and S's have trouble transitioning to life in the B and I quadrants, quadrants where uniting an organization is essential.

From the moment they enter military school, students are taught the importance of mission, the skills of teamwork, and the essentials of leadership—the outer boundaries of the B-I Triangle.

MILITARY SCHOOL

TRADITIONAL SCHOOL

In military schools, it is drummed into students' heads: "Unite to win. Divide to conquer." Military students are trained in the skills to unite, and then to focus the united force to divide and conquer the enemy.

Unfortunately, in traditional schools, students are not taught to unite to win, but only to divide and conquer. Schools train students to compete against their own teammates for grades, class rank, and entrance into colleges. When they leave school, they compete for jobs, promotions, and raises.

This is one reason why so many people get stuck in the E and S quadrants. Success in the B and I quadrants requires leadership skills, the skills to unite people. The ability to unite is essential to leadership in war and in business. Another reason why S's struggle is because they are often competing against organizations operating as a team.

For example, the owner of a small hardware store has a tough time competing against a "big-box" store such as Home Depot.

How to Get Your Upper Hand

If you don't have an upper hand in your business, then it's hard to have much of a business. That upper hand should be based on the little things that count. These are the little things that have given me that advantage and helped me improve my Midas Touch. They can do the same for you.

- **Acquire leadership skills.**
  The U.S. Merchant Marine Academy trained its students to be leaders from the moment we entered the school, day in and day out, until we graduated. Six years as a Marine Corps officer and pilot was also excellent training and leadership development for business.

  Even if you did not go to military school, you can still gain leadership skills at work, in sports, and in civic activities. Leadership is an educational process, a process that challenges you every day. People who avoid leadership and the responsibilities of leadership will probably make poor Midas Touch entrepreneurs. Transitioning from the S quadrant to the B and I quadrants requires leadership skills.

- **Learn how to sell and invest.**
  When I returned from Vietnam in 1973, I decided to follow in my rich dad's footsteps, not my poor dad's. I had one more year on my contract with the Marine Corps, so my rich dad advised me to begin preparing for the S, B, and I quadrants.

  Rather than go back to school and get my master's degree as my poor dad recommended, my rich dad recommended a very different educational path since the skills required for the B and I quadrants are different. Rich dad recommended I learn to sell and invest in real estate before leaving the Marine Corps. He had two reasons. First, entrepreneurs must be able to sell to their customers, their employees, and their investors. If the entrepreneur cannot sell, the business struggles financially. His second reason was that real estate investors must know how to manage and profit using debt. Knowing how to profit from debt was preparing me for the I quadrant.

So in 1973 I signed up for my first real estate investment course. In 1974, I left the Marine Corps and joined the Xerox Corporation to learn how to sell. I worked at Xerox for four years. I left only after I became number one in sales. Both of these educational programs have made me a multimillionaire over and over again. These are skills generally not taught in schools.

- **Hire a coach.**
  The three most important things to me are health, wealth, and happiness. For each of these areas of my life, I have a coach. I know that affording a coach may be difficult, especially if money is tight. Yet, if you are to be a true entrepreneur, you can't afford to let the lack of money stop you. Rather than say, "I can't afford a coach," use your creative mind to find a way to make it happen, especially for the things that are important in your life. If I had allowed my "I can't afford it" thoughts to stop me, I'd be poor, unhealthy, and unhappy today.

- **Don't work for money.**
  I know this sounds strange to most people, yet in these words are the secrets to tremendous wealth. If you have read *Rich Dad Poor Dad,* you may recall that rich dad's very first lesson was: The rich don't work for money. One reason why most E's and S's struggle with money is because they work for money. You're probably wondering, "If I don't work for money, what do I work for? How do I eat and put a roof over my head?" All good questions. Here's the answer.

B's and I's make so much more money because they work to build, buy, or acquire assets. The financial statement pictured below explains the difference.

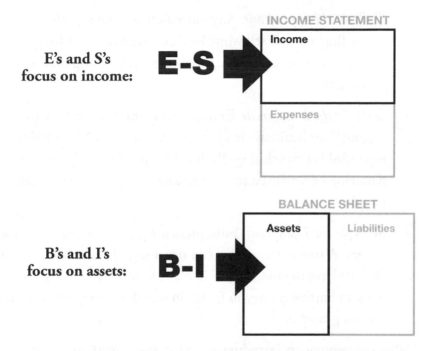

E's and S's focus on income:

B's and I's focus on assets:

Assets include businesses, brands, patents, trademarks, real estate, paper assets, and commodities. Working for assets, rather than money, is a very important small thing that makes a very big difference over the life of an entrepreneur. It gives you the upper hand. The reason is because assets continue to pay you whether you are working or not, and multiple assets can be paying you at the same time. That's how you build wealth. Working for money means you have to work for every hour you are paid. That's not how you build wealth.

Skills You Must Master

In this book, I've referenced the CASHFLOW Quadrant several times. Each area of it requires different skills to be successful. To really excel in the E quadrant, you need many advanced degrees and a strong ability to climb the big corporate ladder.

But if you want to be an entrepreneur, these are the skills you will need to be successful in the S, B, and I quadrants. Master them and you can win. Don't, and you will most likely stay small.

- *Skills for the S quadrant:* Any entrepreneur who says they hate selling or can't sell won't be an entrepreneur for long. Entrepreneurs must be able to sell. It's a little thing that is a very big thing.

- *Skills for the B quadrant:* Entrepreneurs must know how to expand their business via systems. For example, McDonald's expanded via franchising. Rich Dad expanded via licensing. Knowing how to expand is what allows you to leverage what you do.

- *Skills for the I quadrant:* Entrepreneurs must know how to raise money. A true entrepreneur can never say, "I can't afford it," or "I don't have the money." When a real estate investor goes to a bank to borrow money to invest in rental property, the investor is raising capital.

When entrepreneurs learn how to sell in the S quadrant, grow businesses in the B quadrant, and raise capital in the I quadrant, they enter a world few people will ever know. If you are serious about becoming an entrepreneur, then take sales training, search for the systems that can expand your business, and learn how to invest in real estate using debt.

Do Your Own Thing

Here's a word of caution to you that I learned through my own mistakes. Many entrepreneurs fail simply because they want to do their own thing. They enjoy the notion of being rule-breakers who march to their own beat. I was the worst of them. That kind of cowboy mentality is enticing, but unfortunately, business in the S, B, and I quadrants requires discipline. Doing your own thing usually leads to failure or financial struggle.

The fact is that surviving in the S quadrant requires more discipline than surviving in the E quadrant. The S quadrant requires new levels of personal, financial, and business responsibility. When you become an employer rather than an employee, a whole new set of laws—such as labor laws, tax laws, and environmental laws—begins to run your life.

The B quadrant demands higher discipline than the S quadrant. Success in the B quadrant requires a greater focus on systems—such as operations, accounting, employee, finance, legal, and payroll systems. It also requires more talented and higher-paid employees for growth.

The I quadrant requires the most discipline. When raising capital, investment laws from government agencies, such as the SEC, demand much more discipline. Most of the entrepreneurs in jail broke laws in the I quadrant.

In other words, if you want to just "do your own thing," it's best to stay small.

Learn a Lot and Learn Fast

As you know, there is a lot to learn to become an entrepreneur. If you do not like to learn about a lot of different things, and learn fast, it is best to stay an employee or stay small in the S quadrant.

I have a friend who is a chef. She has her own catering company in the wine country of California. She works hard, has a loyal staff of eight, and makes a good income in the S quadrant. The problem is that the only educational classes she takes are more cooking classes. She is always competing against other chefs to win the hearts and stomachs of her customers. She has no interest in studying business or investing. She plans to work hard all her life doing what she loves, and staying small in the S quadrant.

In simple terms, she is doing what she loves, which is to be a chef. But she is not doing what she must do to be an entrepreneur.

As you may have noticed, I believe the biggest little thing for entrepreneurs is the lifelong commitment to education. That counts more than anything else in life and in business. In the real world, it's the people who do what they *need* to do who beat out the people who only do what they *love* to do.

Doing what you must do, even if you do not want to do it, is a little thing that makes a big difference. In every case, that will mean studying and learning about subjects you may not love. Remember, you don't have to be an expert. You just have to know enough to speak the language and eventually hire experts in those subject areas. Most community colleges offer courses in the most vital areas at reasonable prices, and there are countless books and online resources for you to use as well.

If you are committed to the Midas Touch, I recommend the following basic topics for ongoing study:

- **Sales training**

  There is sales training and then there is Blair Singer's sales training. He teaches technique and much, much more. It's the much, much more most entrepreneurs really need.

  Others have had success starting out as part of a network-marketing company where you get real-life sales training.

- **Basic business law**

  It's extremely helpful to have a basic knowledge about the law and how it impacts your business in such areas as intellectual property, labor, environmental, tax, and contracts. This will save you a lot of money and headaches. It doesn't mean you won't need an attorney, but at least you'll be able to speak the language.

- **Basic accounting**

  I teach the importance of the income statement and balance sheet. That's an important start. A basic accounting class will teach you how to start off on the right foot with your business, or get things organized if you're already in business for yourself. Again, you'll still need an accountant.

- **Marketing and advertising**
  Before you invest in marketing and advertising activities, learn as much as you can about them. There's a lot of information out there—in classes and books, as well as online.

- **Web, Internet, and social-networking**
  Take classes and keep up to date on the latest happenings. This area is continually changing. Staying up to speed requires daily reading.

- **People skills**
  Join organizations and networking groups just to practice vital people skills. You have to be able to deal with different people and people with different business skills.

- **Technical investing**
  Take classes on technical investing, aka futures trading. An entrepreneur must know how to make money in markets that are going up, and in markets that are coming down. To simply believe that markets only go up is naïve.

Remember, this isn't about becoming an "A" student in these subjects. Just know how these subjects interact in a business. You do not have to do these courses all at once. Just dedicate your life, over time, to continuously learn these subjects. Your lifelong commitment to learning is a little thing that makes a very big difference. We all know people who will promise to keep learning, but who fail to keep that promise. Keeping this promise is the little thing that counts the most. Remember, entrepreneurship has little to do with what school you went to. Success goes to the entrepreneur who keeps on learning, even when school is out.

A Word about Generosity

Contrary to popular belief, becoming rich in the B and I quadrants requires generosity not found in the E and S quadrants. B's and I's must be generous in order to succeed. E's and S's don't. As a B, you must be willing to make a lot of people rich before you become rich.

To become rich in the I quadrant, you must be willing to share the wealth with investors.

If you are not a generous person, then you may want to begin personal development in that area. You simply must want to make other people money and include them in the bounty of what you are building if you want to have the Midas Touch.

A Final Thought

If I had known how much I had to learn, I might never have started my career as an entrepreneur. It is much easier to be an employee. Yet, in retrospect, becoming an entrepreneur has been the best educational program I have ever gone through—and I continue to learn.

Is it worth it? As hard as the process was and continues to be, for me, it has been well worth it. It has provided me:

- *Unlimited wealth*
  Although it was difficult at the start, today Kim and I have plenty of money to live the life we choose to live.

- *Global freedom*
  Being a global entrepreneur allows me the freedom to do business throughout the world.

- *Great friends*
  Had I not become an entrepreneur, I would not have met great entrepreneurs such as Donald Trump, Steve Forbes, and Oprah Winfrey.

- *Peace of mind*
  Unlike my poor dad who always worried about money or losing his job, I don't. I am no longer a slave to money.

My rich dad often said, "If you gave everyone in the world a million dollars and told them they had a year to spend all of it, most people could complete that task.

"Yet if you asked everyone in the world, 'Starting with nothing, can you acquire a million dollars in a year?' only a very few could. And the few would probably be entrepreneurs."

The world can use a lot more people who can create wealth and, in the process, solve many of the challenges we face. That's what it will take. True entrepreneurs will seldom do it for the money. They nearly always have a higher calling. But when they achieve their own wealth, the freedom that comes with it is what keeps them going and moving on to the next venture.

If I lost all my money, I know I could simply make the money back and keep going with my mission. Having that knowledge may seem like a little thing to most people, yet having this power is a very big thing to me.

I wish the same power for you.

Luxury and Details:
One Small Thing That Became a Big Thing
Donald Trump

Trump Tower was nearing completion, and I wasn't sure what to name it. I told a friend I was thinking of naming it "Tiffany Tower" because of its proximity to Tiffany's. He asked why I'd use someone else's name instead of my own. That was a good point. The alliteration was similar, and so it became Trump Tower. This little thing, a detail that was almost an afterthought, became a big thing as my name eventually became well known. It was the beginning of my brand.

Trump became a big name largely because I brought name recognition to the company, starting with Trump Tower. In essence, I was doing my own advertising with a name and a landmark. Don't underestimate the power of publicity, even if it isn't a huge campaign, no matter what form it takes. When Trump Tower opened, luxurious in every way, it was the beginning of the Trump brand becoming synonymous with luxury. Eventually, the publicity brought fame as well and has made our brand become synonymous with money, power, and luxury. You'll find that your brand will reflect on you, so choose carefully what you want to be known for.

When Small Is Big

Robert couldn't be more correct when he talks about focusing on the little things that count. For the Trump brand, the small thing is people's desire for the nicer things in life—fame, power, and celebrity status. It's a slice of the celebrity life made real through our properties and the products that bear our name. This small thing has become a very big thing for me and The Trump Organization. This seemingly small desire that people have has become the foundation for our entire company. Do you have an idea what that small thing could be for you or your business?

When Robert talks about thinking small, I have to laugh because I've been known for my "think-big" credo. I've never been accused of thinking small, and I take that as a compliment. Big has served me well, but I'm also known for being detail-oriented. Big leads to countless details that require attention. In fact, to be very successful, you have to realize that there are no little things. Everything matters, particularly when you have a brand that is known for luxury. As someone once said, and as I've said before, "A tiny leak can sink a ship."

Robert says that if he lost all his money, he knows he could make the money back again. That represents power to him. He has that power because he is very educated financially and has many experiences to draw upon.

I know the feeling, because I went through a major financial upheaval in the early 1990s, and I survived it. I came back to be far more successful than I had been before—largely from having learned a great deal in the process. I wouldn't want to go through it again, but I realize that it served a purpose.

My CFO, Allen Weisselberg, who has been with me for over 30 years, advises to "operate your day-to-day business as if bad times are always here," which is a great precaution.

When Big Is Big

When you think big, you will automatically trigger more details because details are the major component of making anything big. They are the stepping stones to high quality and a strong structure.

I think in construction terms, and a blueprint is something to consider as you begin your business. Is it a small blueprint? Can it be expanded? Wouldn't it save time to just start with a big blueprint? Many years ago I was quoted as saying, "If you're going to be thinking anyway, you might as well think big." My goal was to build skyscrapers, and you have to think big in that case. To me, it was common sense to be thinking big.

Robert says there is a big difference between "little things that count" and "thinking small." He's right. When I was building Trump Tower, my father couldn't understand why I wanted to use glass when bricks had always worked just fine for him and were less expensive. But my vision was a sleek tower, and glass was one of the details that would make it an exceptional and beautiful building. I know my father was impressed and proud when Trump Tower opened to rave reviews, but there was no convincing him that glass would work better than bricks when I first showed him my plans. I just had to stick to my vision. I had the big picture, and I wasn't changing it. That picture was to make it the best building in Manhattan.

Just as Domino's knew that people wanted pizza fast, I knew that there were people out there who wanted luxurious surroundings and personalized, exceptional service. I was confident that, with attention to the little things, the details, we could deliver on this need.

Every big picture is full of small details. Every big symphony has an amazing number of instruments and very minute details that add up to an incredible sound. When I think big, which is often, you can be sure I'm aware of the myriad little things that we will have to account for. Watching the construction of a building from the foundation up will give you a good idea of what we often take for granted, the particulars that give the building a strong foundation as well as character. There was a point when I would walk up the stairs to the top floor of my buildings (which can be very high) just to get the feel of the building. Of course, I was also checking the condition of the stairwells and everything else, because everything matters— whether it's seen or not. It also kept me and my security guards in pretty good shape.

The Trump Hotel Collection has met with considerable success. We have received the Mobil Five-Star Awards for Trump International Hotel & Tower in New York, as well as *Travel + Leisure* magazine's #1 "Hotel in the U.S. and Canada" award for Trump International Hotel & Tower Chicago. Our hotel in SoHo, New York—Trump SoHo— made *Travel + Leisure* magazine's list of the best new hotels. It was the only hotel in New York that made the list.

What qualifies our hotels for these distinctions? It's our commitment to luxury and then fulfilling that commitment through the little things that matter to our guests. It means attentive service on all levels, and state-of-the-art amenities and conveniences. No detail is too small for us, thus, the big awards. Yes, the hotels are big, but the personalized service is as far from impersonal as you can get. We realize that our guests are expecting a certain level of service, and that's what we give them. Often, on a return visit, they are surprised that we've kept their information and can ask the appropriate questions, such as whether they'll require a babysitter during their stay and other personal requirements. We have a gold standard to attend to, and we do. None of the so-called little things are little to us.

People are surprised to hear that I sign my own checks. That's a lot of checks every week, piles and piles of them. It's one of the little things that can matter. I like to know where my money is going.

I had one job that, for some reason, seemed too expensive, and I was unhappy with the costs. At the time, I was not signing the checks for that job. I got very angry at the people running the job and ultimately said to them, "From now on, I want to personally sign every single check." The minute I suggested that, my costs automatically went down by 15 percent, without negotiating. Now I sign everything.

Books and Skyscrapers

Considering the scope of my projects, people sometimes ask me why I spend time writing books. I don't consider writing books a small venture because I prize education, as does Robert. Writing books is essentially a sharing experience. A lot of people don't want to share their knowledge. A level of confidence is necessary here, but both Robert and I have had the success necessary for an audience to want to know how we think and work. I don't mind sharing my tips for success because I know I will continue to work and succeed. Books can be teaching tools. They may be small items compared with golf courses and skyscrapers, but they can be powerful.

A good example of that is how my first book, *The Art of the Deal*, which came out in 1987, affected Mark Burnett as well as Robert and his wife Kim. Mark was selling T-shirts in Venice Beach, California, when he read it. Robert and Kim were struggling when they read it because they were just starting their new business. Both parties said it made a significant impact on them and steered them towards success. Those are just three examples of how one book can positively affect people.

In the fall of 2008, a citizen in Canada sent me a copy of her local newspaper from Kamloops, British Columbia. There was a photograph of a homeless man who was surrounded by his belongings, and he was reading a copy of *The Art of the Deal*. The photo made me want to help him with his immediate situation.

The homeless man had been told that I'd read his story, and he joked about it, asking if "the cheque's in the mail." He didn't know or believe I'd be sending him one, which I had. When he was handed the check, he said, "For once in my life, I'm speechless. I'm at a total loss for words. Usually I'm so loquacious, but this? I don't know what to say."

My message to give to the homeless man was: "Give him my regards, and tell him to work hard. I know it's not easy out there." To send him a check was a small gesture on my part, but small things can mean a lot. The small things matter.

Another example is when I was watching *60 Minutes* one Sunday night and there was a segment about Maytag moving their plant from Newton, Iowa, to Mexico, and the devastating effect it had on this hardworking town. Three individuals were interviewed and each of them impressed me in one way or another. One was a war veteran, another owned a Domino's Pizza shop, and the third individual owned a product-advertising company. I was impressed by their work ethic and their resolve to not let the economic woes caused by Maytag's departure break their spirit. Again, as a small gesture, I sent two of them a check, one to be used for his daughter's college fund and the second to cover shortfalls at the pizza store. With the third individual, I created an ongoing and continual business to provide me with top-quality merchandise affixed with the Trump brand. It was a small gesture on my part but, at that time in their lives, a positive impact was made.

Visiting My Office

One surprise people get when they visit my office is to hear me on the phone negotiating the price of sinks, chairs, lamps, mirrors, chandeliers, and so forth. I know all the prices, the vendors, and the ins and outs of making deals with them. At the moment, I have approximately 20 mirrors in and around my office as I'm deciding which ones will be best at one of my golf courses. On other days, you might come in to see a variety of chairs on display, or even sinks. I'm very particular about fixtures and want to get a feel for them, along with their pricing and how they look.

My controller, Jeffrey McConney, learned a big lesson early in his career with The Trump Organization. He'd been with me for about six or eight months, and each week he would come in and give me a cash snapshot of how things were going. One week he came in and told me we were down a substantial amount from the week before. Then the phone rang, and I picked it up. During the conversation, I looked up and told Jeff, "You're fired." I hired him back a few minutes later, but the point was made. It was a wake-up call. It's my money, and his job is to protect it. He's now been with me for over 25 years.

Inside The Apprentice

People might think I just show up each week at the boardroom or at the locations used in *The Apprentice* and *The Celebrity Apprentice*. There's a lot of detail work for each episode and I am definitely a part of the process—from casting, to locations, to task assignments, and so forth. The preparation for each season is complex and involves a lot of coordination between the producers and me. I oversee everything— from the opening to marketing, to the cast list, to audition tapes. Months of pre-production and casting are involved. Production comes in two months before the shoot begins. Post-production continues until the last episode airs.

There are some dramas to be considered, usually centering around the boardroom. Once we had an emergency call at 6:00 a.m. when a cast member had been caught cheating. Sometimes the boardroom goes on for five hours, but it's edited down for the episode. Once I showed up in black tie for the boardroom because I had to attend a formal event immediately afterwards. I've learned to multi-task over the years, fitting in business meetings between takes for the show. Since we do a lot of shooting in Trump Tower, I can readily get to and from my office. Sometimes the crew shoots right inside my office. We're used to film crews by now, so it's business as usual in the office.

There are small things that require time and thought that most viewers wouldn't even be aware of, unless they are in the industry. With New York as a backdrop, we have a wonderful selection of sites, but there are many factors to be considered, such as permits, weather, traffic, transportation, and the list goes on. I don't just appear, but deal with many details throughout the shooting season and work closely with Mark Burnett. When the season begins, there is publicity to be considered with television appearances and interviews. It's an ongoing process, and once again, no detail is too small for consideration.

One lesson I learned about the small things was when I was en route to give a speech to about ten thousand people. This was fairly early in my speaking career, and I remember casually asking my driver what I was going to be talking about. He was startled by my question and said, "Boss, don't you know? There are thousands of people waiting for you." I told him that I was sure it would come to me. He didn't seem relieved at my answer.

What I decided to do was to think about the audience as individuals instead of a huge mass of people, and what they might like to hear about. Instead of thinking big, I was actually thinking small. Sure enough, everything became clear and the speech was a great success. I focused on where the audience was coming from, not where I was coming from, and the rapport was tangible. It was a good formula to keep for future engagements and a very good visual aid for those of you who are wary of public speaking.

Trying to Fly the Flag

When I'd finished my golf course in California, Trump National Golf Club Los Angeles which fronts the Pacific Ocean, I decided to fly the American flag on the property. I thought it was the perfect setting for our flag, which it was. The community didn't think so. They said it was too big. "Too big for what?" was my response. "It faces the Pacific Ocean!" Eventually everyone rallied to my side, and the flag now flies proudly on the site. Here was a case of big versus small and small versus big, in the most classical sense possible.

We've been talking about the big and the small, and I often refer to difficult circumstances as being either blips (small) or catastrophes (big). On one hand, every detail is important, but it's also prudent to see that catastrophes include wars, earthquakes, tsunamis, and terrorist attacks, so that our perspective remains intact. Part of our IQ is being able to identify which is which.

If I see our profits taking a big dip, that's not a minor detail by any means, and it would take precedence over negotiating for sinks. But it's also not a tsunami. It has to be dealt with and can be dealt with. It's often been said that being able to prioritize is a skill worth developing.

Cruise Control

I was scheduled to make a short appearance on a boat that was filled with people taking an evening cruise around Manhattan. I arrived at sunset, made some introductory remarks, and did a meet-and-greet with the guests on board. I was busy into conversation when I turned around and realized we had left the dock and were heading down the Hudson River. No one notified me of the departure, and I wasn't too pleased. I hadn't planned on a three-hour cruise around Manhattan! But since there wasn't much I could do about it at that point, I decided to relax, enjoy the great views of the city as well as the nice crowd. It was a very pleasant and inspiring evening for me. Manhattan lit up at night is really worth seeing from the Hudson River. It was a pretty big detail to miss leaving the boat on time, but this was one blip I didn't mind.

Talk About a Detail!

Being able to see locations is also a skill worth having, especially if you are a developer or entrepreneur. Talk about a detail! I remember when I had an option on the property where the Javits Convention Center in New York City now stands. I was instrumental in the development of the Javits Center and knew the project could be done by my company at a cost of $110 million. It ended up costing the city between $750 million to $1 billion.

I offered to take over the project at cost, but my offer was not accepted, which was a huge loss to the city and its visitors on many levels. First of all, the cost was ludicrous, but the result was even more startling. The Javits Center, one of the prime pieces of real estate in Manhattan, rests on waterfront property with wonderful and sweeping river views. However, they built the center so that it faces the street—not the river! Whoever did this wasn't thinking clearly, or wasn't thinking at all. Was the river just a small detail to them, or of no consequence? How was this overlooked? It's just unbelievable to see the results. Seeing the scope of a property and what it has to offer is a detail that cannot be ignored. Maybe too many people were involved, but this oversight is still hard to believe.

Trump Tower is the story of how one little thing became a big thing in naming the building that would later become an iconic skyscraper in New York. As an entrepreneur, I was establishing my brand, and this detail proved pivotal to my future success. In fact, an interviewer once said to me that I had become a brand, and it didn't really bother me. Why? My brand is the best. Why would being the best upset me?

As an entrepreneur, you must be true to yourself. You must believe in yourself and your product. Have confidence, work hard, and keep your focus on the small things that matter while keeping the big picture in mind. It's a recipe that has worked for Robert, and it has worked for me. It will work for you too.

Distilling It Down: Little Things That Count

Ask yourself, "What do you do better than anyone else?" It's an important question, because your answer is the seed of your own "little thing that counts" for your business. To help you shift your focus— which is not easy to do for yourself—let's first look at some big-company examples, and then add a few more examples for illustration purposes. Although there are plenty of small-company examples of little things that became big advantages, the big-companies make it easier for most of us to relate to the lessons.

Here's a review of each big company's little thing.

Walmart's Little Thing

As you probably already know, Sam Walton built the Walmart empire on the one thing he did better than anyone else—low prices. He didn't just lower prices, he started with one discount store in Arkansas and built a global empire. So simple was this plan that everyone easily understood it. For nearly 20 years, Walmart's slogan was: "Always low prices—always." On September 12, 2007, they changed the old slogan to: "Save money. Live better." Different slogan, same little thing.

Domino's Pizza's Little Thing

Robert talked about the little thing that turned the pizza business upside down. In 1960, in a world filled with pizza, Tom Monaghan purchased DomiNicks Pizza, a small pizza shop in Ypsilanti, Michigan, for $75 down and $500 a month. Once Tom understood the pizza business, he built a business around the promise: "Pizza in 30 minutes or less, or it's free." Their jingle once was: "One hot number is all you need. Domino's Pizza delivers! 30-minutes fast or free. Domino's Pizza delivers!" Pizza was transformed for decades.

Mary Kay Cosmetics' Little Thing

Mary Kay Ash founded Mary Kay Cosmetics because she wanted to empower women. She said, "My objective in life is to help women know how great they really are." Although she was a single mom, Mary Kay put herself through college. She was successful in corporate America, but became frustrated with the way businesses held women back.

In 1960, she started Mary Kay Cosmetics with her son and $5,000 from her savings. At the time of her passing in 2001, she had 475,000 consultants all over the world, grossing over $2 billion in sales. Famous for giving away pink Cadillacs to her top performers, she became the biggest corporate buyer of cars, giving away 8,000 pink Cadillacs in 1997 alone. She has been profiled in documentaries and magazines, received countless honors, including induction into the National Business Hall of Fame by *Fortune* magazine, and was named "The Greatest Female Entrepreneur in History" by Baylor University. She also received the prestigious Horatio Alger Award. A very religious woman, she said, "God didn't have time to make a *nobody*, only a *somebody*. I believe that each of us has God-given talents within us waiting to be brought to fruition." Her little thing was her ability to empower women.

Facebook's Little Thing

Mark Zuckerberg launched Facebook from his Harvard dorm room in 2004. Today the company is valued in the billions. While still in high school, Mark developed a program he called "ZuckNet" which connected his father's dental practice to the family home. His stated interest is, "Openness: making things that help people connect and share what's important to them." Although there is much controversy around Mark and the origins of Facebook, there is no doubt that he and his business do connect people, allowing them to share what is important to them. His little thing is that he can connect people better than anyone else.

Take a look at these businesses. In every case, they started small in the S quadrant. From there, they never gave up until they built a business around the little thing that counted. Then they built a business empire in the B quadrant. Once they moved to the B quadrant, professionals in the I quadrant clamored for the opportunity to give them money.

Greedy vs. Generous

As Mary Kay Ash said, "God didn't have time to make a *nobody*, only a *somebody*. I believe that each of us has God-given talents within us waiting to be brought to fruition." In essence, she is talking to all of us. It is up to every entrepreneur to look inside and ask, "What is my gift? What can I give the world?" The Midas Touch is about something much greater than just starting a business to make money or get rich.

Contrary to popular belief, the very rich are not greedy. To become very rich, entrepreneurs must be very generous, giving their gifts to others and sharing their God-given talents. Midas Touch entrepreneurs do not just give to their customers. They also bring the gift of wealth and prosperity to those who work for their business. These entrepreneurs create the jobs and prosperity necessary for a stable economy and a stable world.

Religious faiths teach the principle: "Give, and you shall receive." Many people are not rich because they want to receive more than they want to give. Most people are trained to ask, "How much will you pay me? What are my benefits? How much will I make if I work overtime? How much vacation time do I get with the job? How much do you contribute to my retirement plan? How about sick time? How about personal days off?"

Professionals in the S quadrant may say, "My fee is $150 an hour plus travel expenses. I don't work on weekends. I don't make house calls. With all the hours I have worked on your project, I deserve more money. I can't see you for a month because I am very busy." This is what happens when people are trained to work for money, rather than work to serve millions of people. There is a huge difference between these two frames of mind. One focuses on receiving. The other focuses on giving.

The Little Things You Must Do

Before considering a move to the B and I quadrants, ask yourself the following questions:

- Are you a generous person?
- Do you have something to give to the world?
- Do you have the dedication and drive to build a business for the B and I quadrants?
- Are you willing to make other people's lives richer?

If you answer yes, you have the foundational character for becoming a great entrepreneur. If you are dedicated and have the drive to build a B-quadrant business, the following are a few "little things" you must do.

Must-Do #1: Be a lifelong student of business.
Many small businesses struggle or fail because the entrepreneur is really not interested in business. Instead, they are mainly interested in their area of specialty. Remember the restaurant owner who focused on his craft rather than his business? That's what we're talking about here. Donald is interested in his projects, but he's also intensely interested in his business as a whole. So is Robert.

Many entrepreneurs in the S quadrant are technicians, not business people. For example, doctors are very well-trained technicians. Doctors may be in private practice, but their primary focus is not the business of their practice. It is on seeing patients. Doctors are expected to keep up with reading their medical periodicals, not business magazines. Many doctors routinely attend medical conferences to stay current in the latest practices and techniques, but few attend business conferences or investment seminars.

Lifelong learning means that entrepreneurs must spend time with other entrepreneurs to share and grow from each other's experiences. A great place to meet and study with other entrepreneurs is EO (Entrepreneurs' Organization). EO is a worldwide organization with chapters in most major cities. Members learn on a regular basis through extensive educational programs for entrepreneurs. Through a valuable program called "Forum," entrepreneurs meet monthly in small groups and share business experiences and issues. Together they solve problems and move businesses and lives forward. Countless companies in the EO network have succeeded in starting out as S's and rising to large B-quadrant businesses.

The Rich Dad Company is also developing an ambitious program called GEO (Global Entrepreneurs Organization). GEO will focus on the education, experience, and skills that entrepreneurs need to start an S-quadrant business and then grow it into the B and I quadrants. An advantage of being an entrepreneur is that your business becomes your personal business school as you study business. You've got your company as the laboratory, so dig in and make learning a lifelong journey.

Malcolm Gladwell's *Outliers: The Story of Success* is a book all entrepreneurs should read. *Outliers* explains why people like Bill Gates and groups like The Beatles are beyond successful. It explains why there are very few real "overnight successes." Gladwell says instead that we are the product of hidden advantages, extraordinary opportunities and cultural legacies that shape who we are and the success we achieve. It makes sense then to seek out these things in our lives and learn all we can from them. Leave yourselves open to varied experiences, become a lifelong student of business, and you will be far more successful than most entrepreneurs.

Must-Do #2: Find out who you are.
Entrepreneurs are all unique. One way to build a business and turn it into a brand is to know who you are.

Another book well worth studying is *The Hero and the Outlaw: Building Extraordinary Brands through the Power of Archetypes,* written by Margaret Mark and Carol S. Pearson. This book gives entrepreneurs a better look into themselves and their business.

The book describes the archetypes that exist in mythology and in business and suggests that entrepreneurs and brands represent archetypes. Here are the archetypes with a few characteristics and their respective mottos. Can you figure out which type you are?

- **The Ruler** identifies with the king, queen, corporate CEO, president, senator, mayor, and super-efficient soccer mom. Rulers must take control. It's not about taking care of people. The Ruler archetypes are "control freaks." They believe they should make the rules and enforce them. IBM is a ruler brand; Apple is an outlaw brand. If you identify with the rulers, you probably relate to IBM. If you are an outlaw at heart, you love Apple.

  The Ruler's motto is: "Power isn't everything. It's the only thing."

- **The Outlaw** finds identity outside the prevailing social structure. Some outlaws are romantic figures because they were faithful to deeper and truer values, even if they were outside the law. Zorro and Robin Hood are considered good outlaws. The demonstrators at Tiananmen Square were considered good outlaws to those who love freedom. To the Chinese government, the same demonstrators were considered bad outlaws. Many so-called outlaws are rebels protesting the system.

  Outlaws Bonnie and Clyde are romantic American gangster folk heroes and, at the same time, were vicious bank robbers. So were Billy the Kid and Jesse James. John Wilkes Booth thought he would be a hero after he shot President Lincoln. Instead, he became the focus of one of the biggest manhunts in history.

  Mark Zuckerberg is definitely an outlaw. In 2010, Steven Levy, author of *Hackers: Heroes of the Computer Revolution*, wrote that Zuckerberg "clearly thinks of himself as a hacker." Zuckerberg said, "It's okay to break things—to make them better." Today, Facebook holds "hackathons," programming competitions where contestants solve algorithmic-based problem statements. There's even a Hacker Cup with cash prizes awarded to the winners.

The Outlaw archetype loves to break the rules. It's probably safe to say that most entrepreneurs have a little Outlaw archetype in them.

There is a great movie entitled *The Pirates of Silicon Valley*. It is the story of two young entrepreneurs, Bill Gates and Steve Jobs, and how they "pirated" the biggest new businesses from two Rulers of the business world: IBM and Xerox. (Google the movie, and you'll find an 8-minute video excerpt on YouTube that is well worth watching.)

The motto of the Outlaw is: "Rules are meant to be broken."

- **The Caregiver** is the archetype for those in health care, nursing homes, extended care, hospice, hospitals, health clubs, physical rehabilitation, and pharmaceuticals. Organizations and businesses such as the Red Cross, Mayo Clinic, United Healthcare, and Johnson & Johnson fall under this archetype. Entrepreneurs whose gift is in health and healing start medical practices, home healthcare companies, biomedical companies, and senior-citizen facilities.

  The motto of the Caregiver is: "Love thy neighbor as thyself."

- **The Hero** identifies with courage and is also called "the Warrior" archetype. The military, police and firefighters fall under this category. The Navy SEALs are definitely in this archetype as are the New York police and firefighters following September 11, 2001.

  The motto of the Hero is: "Where there's a will, there's a way."

- **The Innocent** identifies with purity and salvation. Churches and preachers fall under this archetype, as does the Salvation Army. Ivory Snow, a brand of soap, attempted to identify with this archetype, promoting purity, innocence, and cleanliness. The birth of the Christ child, the Holy Grail, Knights of the Round Table, and a little house with a white picket fence all fall into this archetype.

  The motto of the Innocent is: "Free to be you and me."

- **The Lover** identifies with romance and sex. Victoria's Secret is the brand that falls under this archetype most vividly in recent years. In foods, brands like Godiva Chocolates and Häagen Dazs ice cream fit this archetype. Many pop artists like Jennifer Lopez and Beyoncé are classic lover brands.

  The motto of the Lover is: "I only have eyes for you."

- **The Explorer** is for those who identify with independence. Brands such as Patagonia Clothing Company and The North Face are in this archetype. Mountain bikers, hikers, sailors, and travel fanatics align with this archetype.

  The motto of the Explorer is: "Don't fence me in."

- **The Jester** identifies with fun. Comedians obviously are in this archetype. Beer commercials often use the jester archetype to attract customers, using television ads with young men acting goofy. Upstart Internet companies—think Google and Yahoo! years ago—often use this archetype as well.

  The motto of the Jester is: "If I can't dance, I don't want to be part of your revolution."

- **The Regular Guy/Gal** identifies with the average person, the salt of the earth. Politicians with "the common touch" do well with this type. Sarah Palin is using the Regular Guy/Gal archetype to further her career inside and outside of politics. Country-Western music, neighborhood festivals, and labor unions appeal to this person.

  The motto of the Regular Guy/Gal is: "All men and women are created equal."

- **The Sage** is the teacher. Both of us work under the Sage archetype. We are the sages for the world of entrepreneurship and financial education. Other sages are George Washington Carver, Albert Einstein, Socrates, Confucius, Buddha, and Oprah. As you can tell, there are different sages for different people. In the world of the B quadrant, corporate America,

Peter Drucker is one of the sage gurus. In the world of the I quadrant, Warren Buffett is the "Oracle of Omaha." All sages have faith in people that can learn and grow in ways that allow us to all create a better world.

The motto of the Sage is: "The truth will set you free."

Now that you know the different archetypes, ask yourself these questions:

- What is my archetype?
- How can I use my archetype to shape my business?

This is where "Must-Do #1: Be a lifelong student of business" becomes relevant. *The Hero and Outlaw* is the kind of book most S-quadrant entrepreneurs typically do not read unless it happens to be within their specialty. Often the study of business is the study of people and leadership, which is the kind of book this is. If you do not want to read and study, evolving into the B and I quadrants might be difficult for you.

Must-Do #3: Work to acquire assets, not money.
Entrepreneurs who develop their Midas Touch do not work for money. They work to create or acquire assets. If there is one thing you take away from this entire book, let it be this: *Focus on assets, not money.*

Most entrepreneurs do not realize that wealth does not come from work, but from the assets they build. For example, most people know Donald for his real estate—such as luxury condominiums, golf courses, and casinos—which are assets he built. But real estate is not his only asset. Donald's TV show, *The Apprentice,* is an asset. This book is also an asset that he and Robert share. Donald has many other assets that are not real estate.

Robert's businesses build assets, such as games, seminars, and books that are sold all over the world. Robert's real estate and oil businesses bring in money every month, whether he works or not. Robert's investment business acquires apartment houses, gold, silver, and copper mines, golf courses, and oil wells. These are all assets.

Most S-quadrant entrepreneurs work for money, which is why they own a job, not a business. In most cases, if they stop working, their money stops. If you are dedicated to building a business in the B and I quadrants, you must build assets. Assets are what separate entrepreneurs in the S quadrant from entrepreneurs in the B quadrant.

Must-Do #4: Don't put round pegs in square holes.
Most businesses continually put the right person in the wrong position or, worse yet, the wrong person in any position at all. In the Industrial Age, people didn't matter very much to a company. All the entrepreneur had to do was build a factory with an assembly line, hire workers and train them to turn bolts, hang tires, and keep up with the production line. In other words, the line, not the people, determined the rate of production. In the Information Age, things became different. Now people matter. The key to success in the Information Age is not high-speed assembly lines, but high-speed and high-quality human thought working towards a common objective.

In the Industrial Age, sand thrown into the gears of the machine could shut down an entire assembly line. In the Information Age, sand thrown into human thought and human interaction can shut down a company's productivity. For example, an emotional upset in the business is the same as sand thrown into the gears of productivity.

Upsetting people is easy, especially in business. It's guaranteed that if you have two people in a company going at 100 miles an hour, three people going at 20 miles an hour, and one person who is out-to-lunch mentally, there will be upset. On a project, if someone wants to move into action, but others want to do more preliminary research and discuss the project further, there will be upset. These upsets slow business from the speed of thought to the speed of blaming and arguing. This can ultimately bring everything to a standstill, including your Midas Touch.

Humans are not machines. Humans work at different speeds. You cannot just step on a human being the same way you step on a gaspedal. In most cases, if you step on a human being, productivity decreases. People must work together for a company to thrive.

Midas Touch entrepreneurs recognize this. The smart ones seek to know themselves well so they can assemble teams that not only complement them, but work well together. If you don't have that, the little thing that counts, well, nothing else really matters.

One of Robert's favorite tools for getting to know yourself and those in your company is the Kolbe Index from the Kolbe Corp. While there are many personality and preference indexes on the market, the Kolbe Index system has unique features and is especially useful for entrepreneurs. For starters, it measures the three parts of the mind that many ancient philosophers and modern psychologists say we all have: thinking, feeling, and doing.

Thinking
Schools measure a person's IQ, which is an indicator of how well they think.

Feeling
This is a reflection of a person's emotions, desires, attitudes, preferences, and values.

Doing
This is a person's instincts, talents, drive, and mental energy.

Kolbe Indexes are unique because they measure the third part of the mind—how a person naturally and instinctively does things. It measures their mode of operation, their drive, and unique talents.

The old cartoon character, Popeye, often said, "I am what I am." Kolbe Indexes measure who you really are. This awareness allows you to operate at your best, and then find and surround yourself

with people who complement you and fill in the gaps. Once you know your team members' Kolbe profiles, you can put the right person in the right position.

Too often, businesses attempt to make Popeye someone he is not. They hire a project manager and try to make him a sales representative. They hire a sales representative and try to turn her into an administrator. Or they hire the wrong person completely and he or she is a cultural mismatch for the company. Before hiring Popeye, you'd best find out who Popeye really is.

To find out who you are, what you do instinctively and naturally, and what your unique talents are, go to the Kolbe.com website and take the Kolbe A Index survey online. For very little money and in very little time, you will instantly learn a wealth of information about yourself. Once you become more self-aware, invite your team to do the same. It will shed valuable light on your company as a whole.

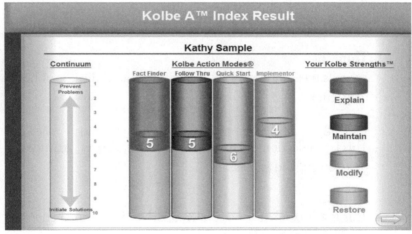

© 2011 Kolbe Corp

Kathy Kolbe, Kolbe Corp founder, says everyone has four different "Action Modes." Depending on our personal index scores, we discover our strengths and learn our most instinctive forms of behavior. The Kolbe Index shows us how to work to our strengths and develop a team that can work well together.

Unlike employees who don't have the luxury of choosing who they work with, entrepreneurs do. It's their most important job. Unfortunately, many entrepreneurs make the mistake of hiring people who have a lot of the same strengths they do.

Entrepreneurs tend to score very high in the Action Mode known as "Quick Start." An entrepreneurial business that hires all Quick Starts will surely have lots of great ideas and get a lot started, but will seldom get much finished. This can lead to customer complaints, incomplete records, shortcuts and, if the dollar amounts are high enough, criminal investigations by the government. Conversely, a business that expects fast motion from a whole team of "Fact Finders" will be very disappointed. They will research and compile data without ever feeling they have enough information to pull the trigger and make a decision.

The reality about the right person for the right job is that business requires people dominant in all four Action Modes. Additionally, business needs people who have no dominance in any one Action Mode. Small businesses, especially one-person operations, are often weak in one or more of the four Action Modes. Big organizations tend to favor one type over the others, so both small and big companies miss out on the additional strengths they need to function well. For example, universities tend to value the natural tendencies of Fact Finders to research before making a decision. They don't value a Quick Start's leap-before-you-look mode of operation.

The Midas Touch Process

You have learned important principles for developing your Midas Touch. Like anything else worthwhile in life, it takes a great deal of effort. For people who are looking for the easy road to wealth, please write a book when you find that road. For both of us, legitimate wealth-building has been neither quick nor simple.

Here are four important steps you must take to evolve into the B and I quadrants. We'll call it the Midas Touch Process.

1. **Become leverageable.**
   S-quadrant entrepreneurs must figure out a way to create leverage in their business. For their business to grow into the B-quadrant, entrepreneurs must leverage their gifts.

Here are a few examples:

- Singers make a record and sell it.

- Personal trainers create a new exercise DVD and sell it via "Infomercials" on television.

- Experts share their knowledge through podcasts that are free to the public, but sponsored by paying companies.

- Programmers create a new application or software program they license to customers.

Your gift is *your* little thing that makes the world better. It is your job to give that gift to as many people as possible. Doing that takes leverage. You can't do it alone. There are only so many hours in the day and the harder you work, the more taxes you pay.

Ask yourself: "How can I leverage my gift to serve more people?"

2. **Become expandable.**
   If it works in New York, works in Phoenix, and works in Columbus, it is expandable to the world. Donald builds luxury all over the world. Robert teaches people about money all over the world. Both men have books that sell all over the world. S's typically have problems expanding. In many cases, the S is a licensed professional like a doctor, lawyer, real estate agent or massage therapist. These professions, and many others, require a license. If they aren't licensed in another city, state or country, they can't do business there. Should they lose their license for any reason, they are out of business entirely. S's are also limited by their inability to be in two places at once. Through leverage, a true B-quadrant entrepreneur can expand to go anywhere and work everywhere. Their motto is: "If there is a will, there is a way." Ask yourself: "What must I do to make my business expandable worldwide?"

3. **Become predictable.**

The more predictable the business, the more valuable it is. Businesses need to be able to predict earnings, expenses, growth, and forecast future revenues and profits. Many of the companies mentioned in this book are masters at predictability. In some cases, they are public companies that are required to forecast. Predictability is why you often hear on market reports, "Apple beat expectations and the stock has hit an all-time high."

But predictability also means consistency of brand experience. Once again, McDonald's is the master of this. No matter where you go in the world, the service, the taste, portion control and the surroundings are very predictable. One problem with S-quadrant businesses is that the entrepreneur is the business. That makes the business very unpredictable. What if the entrepreneur gets sick, injured, burned out or just plain old? The company's ability to continue becomes questionable, and predictability goes out the window. Unpredictability also hits S-businesses when they begin to expand. They often lose control of the little thing they do well. Then predictability declines, and chaos follows. Predictability is not just a nice-to-have. It is critical to securing financing for your business.

Ask yourself: "How far off is my business from becoming predictable, and what must I do to get there?"

4. **Become financeable.**

Once a business can prove its ability to leverage the little thing the business does better than anyone else, investors begin to take notice. When a business proves it can expand and grow, investors become very interested. Once a business achieves predictability, the sky is the limit. That is why Walmart, McDonald's, Apple, Microsoft, and Google are the darlings of the stock markets.

Ask yourself: "Do I have all the pieces in place to make my company financeable? If not, what pieces am I missing?"

The Most Important Thing

Given all the gifts and the little things entrepreneurs can use as foundations to build global businesses, there is one little thing that every entrepreneur must count among their most cherished and important abilities. An entrepreneur's most important little thing is to be an employer who provides jobs for people who are hungry for security, benefits, and a more promising future. It's a massive responsibility and one that Midas Touch entrepreneurs take very seriously. We understand that losing a job has the power to rip out the emotional core of an employee and, in the process, jeopardize their family's well-being. Increased unemployment also affects the communities we live in, our nation, and the world.

The best entrepreneurs believe that the true measure of their success has little to do with their wealth or the size of their homes. It has to do with the number of jobs their business creates. Imagine an entrepreneur like Steven Jobs. His business not only created countless jobs at Apple, but also spurred hundreds of thousands, if not millions, of jobs in all the industries and businesses that support Apple products. That is the Midas Touch.

We must understand that governments cannot create real jobs. Only entrepreneurs can do that. It's up to all of us to take action and change this world for the better.

Points to Remember | Things to Do

- Seek to discover that little thing in your business that can be a big thing to your customers. Uncover your gift.

- Select your tactic and choose strategies to make the tactic happen. Keep it simple and executable.

- Recognize it's your job to focus the mission and bring the B-I Triangle to life.

- The Midas Touch requires discipline. You can be a rebel, but understand that it will demand new levels of personal, financial, and business responsibility

- Be generous with your energy and success. Bring others along for the ride and reward them well. The Midas Touch is not a solo sport. It is a team effort.

- There are no little things, everything matters, so hire wisely and inspire your team with your vision. They will be the ones who carry it out and represent you.

- Think big, set your vision high, and go for it. You'll be shocked by what you can accomplish when you do.

- If it's worth doing, it's worth fighting for. You'll have lots of people and obstacles in your way Work and fight to get beyond them.

- Don't delay. Every day that you work in your business without a vision, without a plan, and without proving it works is another day that you delay your success.

- Discover your true self and surround yourself with people who complement your gifts and modes of operation.

- Commit to being a lifelong learner by studying successful businesses and people to understand the little things that count in their businesses.

- Design your business from the start so that it is leverageable, expandable, predictable, and financeable,

- Realize that an entrepreneur's most important gift to the world is jobs, security, and well-being for others.

- Recognize that the world needs more entrepreneurs. Everyone is counting on you.

AFTERWORD

For centuries, Ellis Island in New York Harbor has beckoned and welcomed the "huddled masses, yearning to breathe free"—men and women from all parts of the world drawn by the beacon of hope and freedom, drawn to "the Land of Opportunity."

Whether these immigrants fled oppression or were drawn by the lure of the American Dream, most viewed this Land of Opportunity as a place for them to stake their claim, make their mark, and create a life of freedom and happiness for themselves and their children. Those tough, ambitious immigrants were willing to do almost anything to gain a foothold, a humble beginning that would become the foundation for the dreams they would build.

Many factors impact the courses that lives take, the way they unfold from one generation to the next, and patterns inevitably emerge. Many first-generation immigrants are willing to pay any price, take any job, shoulder any burden, if there is a chance it will give them a foothold, a start. They do what must be done, for they have come for the opportunity to build the life of their dreams, to give their children something that they themselves never had. And for that, there is no price too steep, no challenge too great, no burden too heavy.

As they hold their children in their arms and dream of the lives their children might enjoy, they instinctively want to spare them the hardships, the often all-too-steep price of freedom. These first-generation children enjoy a different kind of freedom, the freedom and strength that comes from certainty. They know that their parents have survived, even thrived, and have thrown open the doors of opportunity. It is typically this second generation, the children of immigrants, who enjoy the first true measures of freedom in pursuing their dreams, the dreams of entrepreneurs. They embrace all things entrepreneurial and envision a life that is theirs for the making.

As that first entrepreneurial generation sees the fruits of their labor, they aspire for their children to have some of the things they and their parents never had. They see their children earning college degrees and enjoying both status and prestige in becoming professionals, such as doctors and lawyers. As the cycle of change continues, entrepreneurs encourage their children to become the highly educated and well-paid employees that they themselves never experienced. How quickly the yearning for freedom moves to a desire for security and a bid for acceptance and respect.

Ever cyclical, often the children and grandchildren of these doctors and lawyers find themselves yearning for the promise of opportunity and the freedom that entrepreneurs enjoy. They challenge the status quo, and often their parents and grandparents, in pursuit of their dreams.

For where most see obstacles, entrepreneurs see promise and possibility. Rather than cling to security, they choose to embrace opportunity—at all costs, and often, against all odds.

Today, the entire world is open for business. Technology has leveled the playing field and fast-forwarded progress. The geographic barriers that challenged previous generations have all but vanished, and the landscape has grown to encompass unprecedented opportunity. The world today is bright with promise for aspiring entrepreneurs who believe that they can create and shape the future.

Entrepreneurs, driven by their passions and vision, are testimony to the fact that free enterprise and capitalism are alive and well. In a world challenged by change and shaken by uncertainties, we look to the entrepreneurs of today and tomorrow to lead the charge.

Donald J. Trump

Donald J. Trump, Chairman and President of The Trump Organization is the very definition of the American success story, continually setting the standards of excellence while expanding his interests in real estate, sports and entertainment. He is the pre-eminent developer of quality real estate around the world, making the Trump brand synonymous with the gold standard.

His commitment to excellence extends from his real estate holdings to the entertainment industry. From his role as star and co-producer of the NBC hit series *The Apprentice* and *The Celebrity Apprentice* to his award winning golf courses and skyscrapers, his business acumen is unparalleled.

An accomplished author, Mr. Trump has authored over ten bestsellers and his first book, *The Art of the Deal*, is considered a business classic. He received a star on the Hollywood Walk of Fame in 2007. Mr. Trump is the archetypal businessman—a deal maker without peer and an ardent philanthropist.

Robert T. Kiyosaki

Best known as the author of *Rich Dad Poor Dad*—the #1 personal finance book of all time—Robert Kiyosaki has challenged and changed the way tens of millions of people around the world think about money. He is an entrepreneur, educator and investor who believes the world needs more entrepreneurs. With perspectives on money and investing that often contradict conventional wisdom, Robert has earned a reputation for straight talk, irreverence and courage.

Donald Trump and Robert Kiyosaki's first book together—*Why We Want You To Be Rich*—debuted at #1 on *The New York Times* Bestsellers List and sold 500,000 copies in the United States alone.

Index